An Invitation to the Liberal Arts

An Invitation to the Liberal Arts

The What and Why of Classical Christian Higher Education

BENJAMIN P. MYERS

CASCADE *Books* • Eugene, Oregon

AN INVITATION TO THE LIBERAL ARTS
The What and Why of Classical Christian Higher Education

Copyright © 2025 Benjamin P. Myers. All rights reserved. Except for brief quotations in critical publications or reviews, no part of this book may be reproduced in any manner without prior written permission from the publisher. Write: Permissions, Wipf and Stock Publishers, 199 W. 8th Ave., Suite 3, Eugene, OR 97401.

Cascade Books
An Imprint of Wipf and Stock Publishers
199 W. 8th Ave., Suite 3
Eugene, OR 97401

www.wipfandstock.com

PAPERBACK ISBN: 979-8-3852-1936-0
HARDCOVER ISBN: 979-8-3852-1937-7
EBOOK ISBN: 979-8-3852-1938-4

Cataloguing-in-Publication data:

Names: Myers, Benjamin P., author.

Title: An invitation to the liberal arts : the what and why of classical Christian higher education / Benjamin P. Myers.

Description: Eugene, OR: Cascade Books, 2025 | Includes bibliographical references and index.

Identifiers: ISBN 979-8-3852-1936-0 (paperback) | ISBN 979-8-3852-1937-7 (hardcover) | ISBN 979-8-3852-1938-4 (ebook)

Subjects: LCSH: Education, Higher—Religious aspects—Christianity. | Education, Humanistic—Philosophy. | Learning and scholarship—Religious aspects—Christianity.

Classification: LB2325 M85 2025 (paperback) | LB2325 (ebook)

09/22/25

Scripture quotations are from the Christian Standard Bible. Copyright © 2017 by Holman Bible Publishers. Used by permission. Christian Standard Bible®, and CSB® are federally registered trademarks of Holman Bible Publishers, all rights reserved.

For my colleagues present and past.
"Once more unto the breach, dear friends."

The adventure of knowing is our avenue to the adventure of being—to the being of all things *that are*.

JAMES V. SCHALL,
THE LIFE OF THE MIND

We never think entirely alone: we think in company, in a vast collaboration; we work with the workers of the past and of the present.

A. G. SERTILLANGES,
THE INTELLECTUAL LIFE

Contents

Acknowledgments | ix

Introduction | 1

1 Biblical Foundations for the Liberal Arts | 11

2 What Is Man? | 23

3 Why the West? | 35

4 The Necessary Virtues | 48

5 The Myth of the Simple Christian | 63

6 Leadership | 72

7 STEM and the Liberal Arts | 81

8 The Liberal Arts and the Major | 88

Conclusion: The Liberal Arts in Our Time | 99

Bibliography | 105
Subject Index | 107
Scripture Index | 111

Acknowledgments

One of the central arguments of this book is that truly educated people think *for* themselves but never *by* themselves, and it is certainly true that I could never have written this book without the inspiration and wisdom provided by great writers on education from Plato to Mortimer J. Adler. Many of these debts are acknowledged in the footnotes, but many more are dispersed throughout the general disposition of the book and its author.

Nor could I have written this book without many rich conversations with my colleagues in OBU's Western Civilization sequence and OBU's Great Books Honors Program. I am particularly grateful to the following colleagues and former colleagues for indulging me with long discussions of the liberal arts and Great Books education: Jonathan Callis, Brent Newsom, Alan Noble, Karen Youmans, Andrew Armond, Tawa Anderson, Lindsey Panxhi, John Powell, Jessica Rohr, Randy Ridenour, Daniel Spillman, Chris McMillion, Jonathan Ashbach, and Paul Sanchez.

Among my own teachers, this book bears the influence especially of David Strain and William Eakin, although I am confident they could find in it much to interrogate and to correct.

An even greater debt of gratitude is due to my parents, Paul and Ann Myers, who first taught me a love for books and a reverence for the past, and to my wife, Mandy, who collaborates with me every day on shaping the hearts of our children for the True, the Good, and the Beautiful.

Acknowledgments

Above all I am grateful to God, who calls us to himself when he calls us toward Wisdom.

Introduction

WELCOME

As the director of a university program, I meet with a lot of potential college students and their parents. They have a lot of questions about things like the cafeteria, the dorms, and social activities. They also ask more important questions: *What kind of education should I pursue? What kind of education do I want? What kind of education do I want for my children?* These are fundamental and pressing questions about education, but they are also inquiries that can be answered only after other, more foundational questions have been addressed. *What do I value? What do I believe to be the nature and purpose of human beings? What do I seek as the highest good?* These bigger questions should determine the educational path we choose. Yet far too often we separate out the first set of questions from the second set, as if the kind of knowledge we should seek in life has no connection to our reason for existing.

"But seek first the kingdom of God and his righteousness, and all these things will be provided for you," Jesus says (Matt 6:33). The purpose of education should follow from the purpose for life. If the goal of life is simply to make as much money as possible and live comfortably, then an education focused on financial achievement makes sense. If, however, the purpose of human beings is, in the words of the seventeenth-century statement of faith known as the Westminster Shorter Catechism, "to glorify God, and to enjoy him forever," then our education should be expected to give us more than a means of financially supporting ourselves. Our education should give us a way to seek the establishment of God's kingdom in our lives and in our world.

This book is an invitation to a kind of education that will equip us with those kingdom-building means and that has deep roots in the Western tradition. This form of education is inseparable from the history of the Christian church in the Western world. This book is an invitation into the kind of education that, until the twentieth century, was quite simply what was meant by the very word *education* when applied to undergraduate studies. It is an invitation to a form of learning that makes its chief goal the shaping of our affections, by which I mean the aiming of our love toward God through valuing his gifts of truth, goodness, and beauty. This book is an invitation to a great adventure in learning.

WHAT ARE THE LIBERAL ARTS? SEVEN DISTINCTIVES

The kind of education we today refer to as a liberal arts education has its roots in the ancient Greco-Roman world, but it came into fuller being in the medieval period as Christian scholars sought to prepare for a life in service to God and his church through broad and deep learning. Making use of ancient thought—especially the great philosophy of Plato and Aristotle—they learned to "spoil the Egyptians," a phrase found in the works of several early Christian thinkers. They meant by this phrase that, just as the Hebrews took with them the gold of the Egyptians when they made their exodus (Exod 12:36), so the Christian scholar can make great use of the wisdom found among the ancient pagans. The insight and beauty in the ancient tradition is the "gold" the children of God can appropriate from among the pagans. We have simply to knock on the doors of ancient thought. Medieval intellectual leaders in the church believed that the ancient pursuits of rhetoric, philosophy, poetry, history, mathematics, astronomy, and music can be ways of drawing closer to the one creator God who is the source of all that is true and good and beautiful. One of the greatest of the early Christian scholars, Augustine of Hippo, thus speaks in his classic memoir, the *Confessions*, of how reading the *Hortensius*, a book by a pagan Roman orator and philosopher named Cicero, sowed in the young Augustine a love of wisdom that eventually led him to the love of Christ. Cicero was a pagan Roman who lived and died before the birth of Christ, but his love of wisdom was infectious. And once Augustine was infected with the love of wisdom, he did not stop seeking until he found, and was found by, the source of all wisdom, God. All true wisdom leads to God.

As universities developed in the Middle Ages, they came to focus their curriculum largely on the "seven liberal arts," which they divided into what they called the *trivium* and the *quadrivium*, Latin words we might translate as "the three roads" and "the four roads." Students concentrated first on the *trivium*, which consisted of the three subjects of grammar (primarily Latin grammar, and later Greek and Hebrew as well), rhetoric (the art of persuasion), and logic (which is sometimes called "dialectic" and which includes not just formal logic for argumentative purposes but also philosophy itself). The four subjects of the *quadrivium* were the number-based disciplines of geometry, arithmetic, astronomy, and music. All seven of these disciplines were founded on the works of the classical Greek and Roman writers and philosophers but were also subject to the truth revealed in Scripture. Having mastered these subjects, a student was ready for the study of theology, which the medieval university considered the queen of the academic disciplines. At many universities, students also had the opportunity to pursue studies in either medicine or law. These advanced studies—whether theology, medicine, or law—were all conducted on the firm foundation provided by a liberal arts education in the *trivium* and *quadrivium*.

This history still informs how the liberal arts are pursued today, but liberal arts study in our time does not require a rigid duplication of the seven subjects studied in the medieval university. In fact, today's liberal arts student can expect to study far more than seven subjects. In a liberal arts university today, you might take courses in history, philosophy, poetry, psychology, algebra, calculus, and many, many other subjects. Perhaps each of these subjects is traceable in some way back to the *trivium* or the *quadrivium*, but modern liberal arts education is not narrowly confined to a rigid understanding of the original categories of study. A Christian liberal arts education in today's world seeks to duplicate the aims rather than the exact procedures of the *trivium* and the *quadrivium*. The exact courses have changed, but, in a true liberal arts college, the spirit of medieval education lives on in more than just the elaborate robes professors wear for graduation each year.

What the aims of a liberal arts education are is a question I will be answering throughout this book, but it will be helpful to lay out a few simple distinctives of such an education to get us started. While there are many approaches to the classical liberal arts, this list will give you some sense of the indispensable components of a true liberal arts education:

1. A liberal arts education values the past and tradition, and thus it includes deep and sustained engagement with the history of the Western world, which is to say with the history of the culture we live in today. It does not focus narrowly on the current age but rather reaches back in time for the rich resources of thought and feeling found in former ages in order to give the student greater access to truth, goodness, and beauty. A liberal arts education passes on a cultural heritage to its students and instills in them respect for the past.

2. A liberal arts education includes a non-utilitarian treatment of even those subjects, such as science and math, that are often valued solely for their usefulness to technology and industry. What I mean by "non-utilitarian" is that it treats knowledge not just as a tool to manipulate the world but also as a means to enrich the student's soul and to glorify God. A liberal arts education is deeply practical but it is not limited to practicality, nor does it consider everything that is not immediately practical to be frivolous. In short, a liberal arts education treats students as if they have souls.

3. A liberal arts education entails a commitment to truth as an objective reality. It does not accept the intellectual fads of the moment as guiding principles for its curriculum or conduct but rather seeks permanent truth as a foundation for values and actions. A liberal arts education is not neutral on matters of truth but rather encourages its students to humbly but earnestly and enthusiastically seek after what is true.

4. A liberal arts education prepares its students for virtuous and free citizenship, especially in the context of the American constitutional republic. A liberal arts education helps build the resources both of reason and of historical knowledge that are necessary for virtuous and active participation in a republic. Our education is about more than our own fulfillment and ambition. It is about meeting the great responsibilities that come with citizenship.

5. A liberal arts education seeks to impart not just skills, or even just knowledge, but also virtue. It is more concerned with who the student is than with what the student does for a living, though it is far from indifferent to the Christian concept of *calling*. A liberal arts education is *formative* in the sense that it helps to shape the character of the student.

6. A liberal arts education is committed to, and encourages a commitment to, transcendence. It does not treat temporary things as if they are permanent or permanent things as if they are temporary. Thus, a liberal arts education shapes the affections of the student, teaching the student to love what is truly lovable.

7. A liberal arts education acknowledges theology as the "queen of the sciences." In the liberal arts tradition as it was formed in the Christian world, all other academic disciplines are subservient to the goal of knowing God and serving him.

Though there are many secular educational institutions today still referring to themselves as "liberal arts" schools, all seven of these distinctives I have laid out are arguably controversial in the secular academic world today. The seventh distinctive is entirely unthinkable in most modern universities. These distinctives are, however, of fundamental importance for the liberal arts as education as it developed in the Christian West in the medieval period and as it was further developed and augmented during the Renaissance (fifteenth through seventeenth centuries) and the Enlightenment (eighteenth century). All seven aspects of the liberal arts are necessary for any institution to call itself, with any integrity, a liberal arts college or university.

To sum up these seven distinctives, we might say that the purpose of a liberal arts education is to equip you through learning to "Love the Lord your God with all your heart, with all your soul, and with all your mind" (Matt 22:37) and to "Love your neighbor as yourself" (22:39). The liberal arts prepare students for a lifetime of practicing the command given in Phil 4:8: "Whatever is true, whatever is honorable, whatever is just, whatever is pure, whatever is lovely, whatever is commendable—if there is any moral excellence and if there is anything praiseworthy—dwell on these things." Scripture calls us to "dwell on," or ponder, things worthy of our attention. To put that another way, a liberal arts education is greatly about gratitude and the accompanying sense of wonder. This sense of wonder is augmented and strengthened through the inheritance of our cultural legacy, which is a legacy of the Christian intellectual tradition and its place in the Western world.

TWO METAPHORS FOR THE LIBERAL ARTS

As ancient rhetoricians knew, a metaphor can be a good way of making a complicated idea more immediately graspable and apparent. The following two metaphors will help us to think about the value and beauty of a liberal arts education.

Imagine you just made a wonderful, delicious cake. The icing is sweet, but not too sweet. The cake is moist. The whole thing is beautifully decorated with flowers and swirls or, if you prefer, with finely crafted reproductions of all the most important droids from

Introduction

Star Wars. You carefully, lovingly slice the cake and put it on plates to serve to your loved ones. How do you hope they will react?

How would you feel if they sat down and began to eat, finished off the cake in a few giant bites, and then stood up and left without saying a word? Even if they clearly enjoyed the cake, surely you would be hurt by their ingratitude. You would want them to at least express thanks for the beautiful cake you have just served them. You would expect them at the very least to say "thank you." That seems like a minimum expectation.

But, as much as it may be appreciated, is that mere "thank you" the best scenario for you, the baker? You would definitely be gratified by their gratitude, and gratitude would definitely be appropriate. Is gratitude, however, all that you would expect? Isn't there something more? Wouldn't it be far more gratifying if they began to ask you questions about the cake? *How did you get the icing just the right amount of sweet? How did you get the batter to come out so moist without under-baking it? How did you make R2-D2's little lights blink like that?* The baker of the cake is honored in the questions of those who eat the cake. Even the master baker who refuses to reveal his or her secrets is pleased to be asked. The curiosity about the creation is a kind of high praise for the creator.

This kind of praise is one reason the liberal arts matter. God has masterfully made the world, and to ask questions about the world he has made is to honor him as its creator. A life of learning is a life of worship. It is a life of wonder. To learn beyond the confines and demands of strictly "necessary" knowledge is to praise our creative God of abundance. We should think of our education as an act of worship.

There are, of course, many ways one can engage in this kind of worship. Simply lying on one's back and gazing up at the night sky can be such an act of worship. So too can developing a craft—such as woodworking or cake baking—if done in the right spirit. But no human endeavor pursues this form of worship with more intentionality, breadth, and focus than does Christian liberal arts education. A good education should tutor us in wonder and draw us deeper into awe of our creator God.

An Invitation to the Liberal Arts

In our world today, education is treated primarily as something one does for one's own benefit. We are told that we should educate ourselves so that we can get a good job, or build an impressive career, or just vaguely somehow "improve" ourselves. Sadly, even many Christian who have learned in so many other areas of life to take up their cross and follow Christ still arrive at college primarily interested in what the next four (or five) years are going to do *for them*. But the liberal arts tradition is not just another self-improvement scheme. It is certainly not simply preparation for material success. It is, rather, an invitation to a life of worship rooted in the God-centered practice of contemplation, dwelling on things. A Christian should seek to worship God in all he or she does. Why would education be excluded from such a life of worship?

Contemplation, once seen in the Christian world as the highest activity in human life, is rarely viewed as doing much of anything at all in the modern world. The very word perhaps conjures images of worthless mystics sitting on mountain tops and gazing at their navels. The world we live in favors the "man of action." But this was not always the case. Among medieval Christians, the contemplative life was held to be the most desirable kind of life, because it is the life spent cultivating one's love for God. The liberal arts today do not ask a student to completely withdraw from the world, or at least not for more than four years or so. You don't have to be a monk or a nun to get a liberal arts education. But the liberal arts do cultivate the habits of contemplation—that is, of reason and thoughtfulness—that prepare one to live meaningfully. The liberal arts invite one to ponder truth, goodness, and beauty and thus arrive at a wonder that is really the worship of our great creator God. Through study we are shaped to be more thoughtful people.

But it is hard to cultivate the kind of understanding and appreciation that leads to wonder on our own. We need resources for such thinking. We need help from great minds that have gone before us. We need material to think about. We need to think *for* ourselves but not *by* ourselves. Thus, let's consider another metaphor.

Introduction

My family and I live in a house that is, by the standards of our part of the world, quite old. It was constructed the same year our home state of Oklahoma was granted statehood, 1907. It is a beautiful old house, if I may say so myself. It has high ceilings and large rooms with beautiful decorative woodwork. It has a large porch wrapped around the front and one side and another porch in back, giving us a variety of comfortable places to sit on days of pleasant weather. There is a balcony on the front and a lovely staircase that leads from the entry room up to a second floor, where the bedrooms and a spacious hallway are found. With more than four thousand square feet, it has plenty of room for our family of five to spread out, but it also has lots of cozy nooks for reading or snuggling up to watch a movie. Moreover, it is in a lovely historic neighborhood within a short walk from a coffee shop, a movie theater, and a drug store. In short, it is a home that is both functional and pleasant.

Now here's the kicker: we did not buy this house. In fact, the simplest way to put it is that we inherited it. The home belonged previously to my wife's parents, though they did not live in it but, rather, ran it as a bed and breakfast. When my mother-in-law decided she no longer desired to operate it as a business, we were offered the house as a kind of early inheritance. We were happy to move in. We did nothing to build the house. It became ours simply because we were the next generation to come along.

We are more than happy to enjoy the pleasant amenities of the house. We are blessed also to enjoy its rich aesthetic offerings, to live in and with its beauty. It is a blessing to have the house. But it is also a great responsibility. Consider what kind of people we would be if we simply enjoyed the house, used it up, and let it fall apart. Consider what a waste and shame it would be if we, who inherited this useful and beautiful old home, were to leave our own heirs homeless.

By now, my metaphor has become obvious. To become educated in the classical liberal arts tradition is to step into a rich inheritance of thought, beauty, and history. Our culture—an appreciation for it at its best and an understanding of it even at its worst—gives us a place in which to live. We might survive, but we cannot thrive in the barbaric wilds of an eternal present tense. Perhaps you have heard someone say, or have even been told yourself, to "live in the moment." This is very common advice in our world and is the moral of many movies and television episodes. But the moment is a terribly small and cramped place to live. We need more room than the moment can provide. The human mind and soul, to be well, must spread out in time. We need resources of thinking and feeling beyond what our own moment in time can supply. We need a house with many rooms, some of which may be in disrepair but many of which are still beautiful and call for our appreciative attention.

How arrogant and foolish to think that our particular moment in time has a monopoly on truth and insight. To think well, we need to think along with the great thinkers of the past. We also need to take responsibility for maintaining that heritage of thought and experience so that it can be utilized by future generations. We must keep well the house we have inherited. It is our responsibility to pass it on.

The invitation in this book is an invitation into that grand house. It is an invitation to sit and to eat the cake and to linger over discussion of the recipe. It is an invitation to a long-standing, firmly rooted, and distinctly Christian form of education that is often quite at odds with the values and assumptions of the world around us. If you are on the verge of deciding where to go to school, I hope this book will help you to see the soul-enriching value of the liberal arts. If you are a parent of a soon-to-be college student, I hope this book will help you to recognize what it is you want your son or daughter to gain from the next four years. If you are a student newly enrolled in a liberal arts college or university, I hope this book will help you understand the kind of adventure you have already set out upon and will help you value that adventure as a part of your walk with Christ. If you are a new faculty member at a liberal arts school, I hope you too will find in the following pages an invitation to a great adventure in kingdom building. Enter the house and claim your inheritance. Sit and eat.

I

Biblical Foundations for the Liberal Arts

THE IMPLICIT "CHRISTIAN" IN THE LIBERAL ARTS

As a college professor part of my job is to attend various yearly conferences to hear and to give presentations in my academic discipline. Some of these conferences are aimed especially at Christian scholars, but many of the conferences I attend are sponsored by secular universities or secular academic associations. A few years ago while attending one very large yearly gathering for professors and students of creative writing, I found myself at an evening reception and poetry reading, chatting with a group of professors from various institutions around the country. When asked the very common question about where I teach, I naturally responded by naming my home institution, Oklahoma Baptist University. Imagine my surprise when another professor in the group responded with a smirk and the question, "Oh, is that near Jesus State University?" To this professor, the very idea of a Christian education was clearly odd and comical. His clear intention was to mock what he saw as my quaint and oddball university affiliation.

An Invitation to the Liberal Arts

Yet, in the historical big picture, it is his secular university, and the type of highly specialized and career-oriented education that happens there, that is the oddity. The particularly rude professor I was talking to seemed not to know that Christian education has been the norm in the Western world for over a thousand years and that the church established the foundation for education as we know it in the modern world.

The liberal arts arose within the Western university while universities were still extensions of the church in the West. This relationship between the church and the university lasted as the dominant—in fact almost sole—paradigm for education in the Western world well into the modern age. It was not until the end of the eighteenth century that secular colleges—with UNC Chapel Hill among the first—began to appear in America. Thus, while today many people think that Christian universities are the oddball, it is, in fact, secular education which is the historical anomaly. For most of the history of higher education in the West, what was meant by "the liberal arts" was the *Christian* liberal arts.

Before secularization had thoroughly reworked education in the modern age, colleges existed primarily to serve the intellectual and pastoral needs of the church, and they met these needs through the liberal arts, from the founding of Oxford in the eleventh century, to the founding of Harvard in the seventeenth century, to the founding of Oklahoma Baptist University in the early twentieth century. When, for example, the pre-revolutionary legislature in Connecticut passed legislation for the establishment of Yale, they prefaced the act in this way:

> Whereas several well disposed, and Publick spirited Persons of their sincere Regard to & Zeal for upholding & Propagating of the Christian Protestant Religion by a succession of Learned & Orthodox men have expressed by Petition their earnest desires that fully Liberty and Priveledge be granted unto Certain Undertakers for the founding, suitably endowing & ordering a Collegiate School within his Majties Colony of Connecticot wherein Youth may be instructed in the Arts & Sciences who

thorough the blessing of Almighty God may be fitted for Publick employment both in Church & Civil State.[1]

Thus, it is easy to see that the liberal arts, though sending roots back into ancient thought, arose out of a distinctly Christian worldview. The liberal arts were shaped by the unique Christian view of reality, and they still bear that stamp of Christianity today.

Without the Christian faith as a foundation, advocates of the liberal arts struggle to justify themselves in the secular educational context. The secular so-called liberal arts are a ghost without a body. Many secular colleges don't know how to explain their purpose, and many secular colleges that refer to themselves as liberal arts colleges are simply nothing of the sort. They may have begun by offering a liberal arts education under the widespread influence of Christianity, but under coercion from modern values of efficiency and materialism, their core curricula have declined into a cafeteria smattering of options or into mere "gen-ed" courses meant to prepare one solely for taking on the more serious work of the major.

Other institutions still offer a somewhat coherent core but do so only by running on the fumes of a faith they no longer embrace. Colleges of this sort find few resources for defending their curricula when challenged by either practicalities or postmodern political pressures. Thus this second sort of secular liberal arts college is usually found in a state of transition into the first kind. For most small colleges secularization and the abandonment of meaningful and robust liberal arts education go hand in hand. A few smaller secular colleges retain a strong liberal arts identity by maintaining strong ties to faith traditions despite their officially secular status. These institutions tend to emphasize the usefulness of the liberal arts for an informed and virtuous citizenship and, despite having no official church affiliation, seem never to be far from the thinking of important Christian figures such as Augustine, Thomas Aquinas, Martin Luther, and C. S. Lewis.

---

1. Yale Corporation, *Charter and Legislation*, 4.

An Invitation to the Liberal Arts

If the liberal arts are an inherently Christian enterprise, arising out of a distinctly Christian worldview, it should not be surprising that the Bible provides an ample foundation for that kind of education we are discussing. A thorough search of the Scriptures reveals much on the topic of education directly or that has clear implications for education. Moreover, Scripture does not leave us neutral on the nature of education but rather suggests that the kind of formative experience supplied by a liberal arts education benefits the individual believer in his or her walk with Christ and benefits the church as a whole in its role as Christ's representative on earth.

WHAT GOD HAS SAID

In the last chapter I mentioned several important passages of scripture that invite us to the kind of life pursued through a liberal arts education. In this chapter I want to discuss those passages further and consider some key concepts from Scripture that provide a foundation for the liberal arts. I will endeavor not to wrest these passages out of context but rather to understand them as the spirit intends. That means that I will not pretend that they are descriptive of the liberal arts as they developed in the two thousand years since Christ's incarnation. Rather, they prescribe a kind of Christian formation, a kind of discipleship which partners with the sanctification of the spirit to mold us for Christlikeness. This Christian formation may be accomplished in a number of ways, but it has been accomplished historically—and is most likely accomplished most fully—by Christian liberal arts education as it has developed in the centuries following the birth of Christ. In fact, I see the development of the liberal arts tradition in the West as part of God's provident care for his people. Of course, no verse in the Bible explicitly commends, much less commands, a liberal arts education. The Bible does, however, prescribe for the Christ-follower a life of thoughtfulness, gratitude, and love for the lovely. These are the biblical aims that inform the authentic liberal arts tradition.

For any discussion of education, Proverbs is a very good place to start. The Proverbs have a lot to say about what we should seek intellectually, and what that is, in short, is *wisdom*. Throughout the Proverbs we are told to seek wisdom above all earthly things. We are accustomed to arguing that wisdom is all well and good but one has to pay the bills, after all. Proverbs, however, sets very different priorities:

> Get wisdom—
> how much better it is than gold!
> And get understanding—
> it is preferable to silver. (Prov 16:16)

I don't quote this proverb merely to thrill the heart of those in charge of collecting the tuition but rather to point out that biblical priorities are at odds with worldly priorities. The world says to make sure first you have all your worldly needs and comforts met. The Bible, on the other hand, says to seek God's kingdom first, to prioritize godly wisdom. Biblically, the pursuit of wisdom is not a hobby for the few who find themselves strongly inclined to it. Rather, it is presented as part of the path of holiness. The pursuit of wisdom is mandatory, not optional, for the Christian life. But how are we to find this wisdom?

Setting such a godly priority means, of course, practicing spiritual discipline and being involved in the life of the church, but it also has deep implications for the kind of education a Christian person chooses to pursue. When we say that we will rely on Bible study class on Sunday mornings and the occasional Wednesday discipleship meeting—or perhaps just Christian radio and spiritual self-help blogs—to pursue godly wisdom but aren't willing to make the pursuit of such wisdom part of our college education, then we are attempting to keep that pursuit on the margins of our lives. We are separating out the pursuit of wisdom, giving it the smallest window, and then pursuing our real priorities with the bulk of our time. We are treating wisdom like something extra to be added only if all other priorities are met already. But that is not the biblical model, and to neglect the pursuit of wisdom *as a priority* is to ignore the clear meaning of Scripture. The third chapter of Proverbs contains another passage that establishes priorities:

> Happy is a man who finds wisdom
> and who acquires understanding,
> for she is more profitable than silver,
> and her revenue is better than gold.
> She is more precious than jewels;
> nothing you desire can equal her. (Prov 3:13–15)

To dismiss this passage as irrelevant to education is to dismiss it entirely, to ignore the word of God. The Lord has commended to us a life in search of wisdom. This wisdom, of course, can and should be sought in multiple areas of life, both individually in spiritual discipline and collectively as a church body. But to exclude its pursuit from such a centrally important, foundational, and prolonged experience as college education is to demote it below the practical considerations of life, as if man lived by bread alone.

But what is this *wisdom* the Proverbs speak of? The Hebrew word *hokma* carries with it associations of knowledge and insight but also of both craftsmanship and virtue.[2] What these associations seem to add up to is wisdom as a vision of the true order of things and as a way of life that confirms itself to the true order of creation. This is what we are being told through the poetry of Proverbs 9: "Wisdom has built her house / she has carved out her seven pillars" (Prov 9:1). Medieval thinkers such as Albert the Great associated the seven pillars of wisdom's house with the seven liberal arts, but we need not be so specific to see that the personification of Wisdom in Proverbs offers us wisdom not as a mere tool to be used but as a dwelling in which to make a life. Remember the second of our metaphors from this book's introduction? Wisdom is not a means to a "lifestyle" but rather is a way of life centered on truth, goodness, and beauty. The pursuit of wisdom is the building of a house to live in mentally, emotionally, and spiritually. In the complex and deceitful fallen world, such a building requires the solid foundation of an education that puts wisdom first.

---

2. Waltke, *Book of Proverbs*, 76–78.

When we consider the vision of wisdom presented in the Proverbs, we see that there is perhaps no passage of scripture more relevant to education than Phil 4:8, a passage that tells us much about how to build a house for the wise. As Paul is drawing to a close his letter to the first church planted in Europe, after having given much precious guidance regarding perseverance in the Christian life and unity in the young church, he gives a charge that should be the center of every Christian education:

> Finally brothers and sisters, whatever is true, whatever is honorable, whatever is just, whatever is pure, whatever is lovely, whatever is commendable—if there is any moral excellence and if there is anything praiseworthy—dwell on these things. Do what you have learned and received and heard from me, and seen in me, and the God of peace will be with you. (Phil 4:8–9)

This verse often gets reduced to an easily digestible lesson along the lines of "don't watch dirty movies." Such a moral, a guarding of the heart through a guarding of the mind and eyes, is, in fact, an important thing to understand in Paul's message. But we should not overlook the fact that the direction is not given in the negative. It is not a *thou shalt not* but rather a *thou shall*. Paul gives us good warrant to avoid corruption—vulgarity, pornography, cruelty, and the like—but he also tells us where to direct our attention instead. Thus, it is worth taking some time to examine the list he provides.

The first thing Paul tells us to dwell on is "whatever is true." It should come as no surprise to any Christian that we have an obligation to seek truth. Throughout especially the Gospel of John, truth is associated directly with our Lord Jesus. Jesus tells us that he is himself the truth (John 14:6) and that knowing the truth will set us free (John 8:32). When we acknowledge this close association between Christ and truth, we see that truth is not just a means to an end—that old idea that "knowledge is power"—but rather is something to be valued for its own sake. The truth is sanctified by Christ's claim on it.

One, of course, does not need a liberal arts education to grasp the fundamental truth of the gospel: that Jesus, the very divine Son of God, died for our sins and was resurrected that we may be redeemed in him and reconciled to our perfect and holy Heavenly Father. This truth is graspable by the child, the mentally handicapped, the uneducated, and even the willfully ignorant. But Paul doesn't limit his direction to this knowledge, as fundamental and essential as it is. There is a next step. He tells us to dwell on *whatever* is true. This is an acknowledgment of how its association with Christ sanctifies—that is, makes holy—all truth. When we learn about creation, whether we explore the created order through biology, algebra, or Italian poetry, we know the creator better. Under the direction of the Holy Spirit, Paul is telling us to seek God through seeking truth. He is telling us to know God better simply by knowing his creation more. This is, of course, a direction to think theologically, but it is not a direction to think only about the academic discipline of theology. It is a commendation of truth itself, in all aspects of life.

A Christian worldview thus rejects the purely instrumentalist or "utilitarian" view of knowledge which says that knowledge is only good when it is useful for some particular, practical enterprise. This view usually associates knowledge with the getting of money. It is, of course, not bad to use knowledge in the pursuit of an honorable living. The good carpenter uses knowledge of wood types, tools, and techniques to build a cabinet. The good accountant uses knowledge of arithmetic, spreadsheets, and tax regulations to keep accurate books. The good lawyer uses knowledge of the law and precedent to represent the client well or to pursue justice. These are very good uses of knowledge. But the Christian view is that truth is valuable beyond its practical uses. You may sometimes hear this idea expressed by educators through the phrase "knowledge for knowledge's sake," but I believe that phrase is inadequate. What we really ought to say is "knowledge for the sake of the glory of God." Part of what Paul is gesturing toward in Phil 4 is something like the metaphor of the cake I used in the introduction to this book. We honor God when we seek to look into the true nature of things, to know the facts about nature, about humanity, and about the cosmos.

If Paul points us back to the cake metaphor, he also points us back to the metaphor of the inherited house, as he directs our thoughts to not just whatever is true but also whatever is honorable, commendable, excellent, and worthy of praise. He is in essence telling us to value what is truly valuable, to love what is lovable. In the liberal arts tradition this goal is often spoken of as the "shaping of our affections." A classical liberal arts education in the Christian tradition helps the student to identify what the author Russell Kirk, following the great poet T. S. Eliot, often called "the permanent things." The liberal arts are designed to introduce students to the great books, the big ideas, the important concepts, and the defining moments that have shaped the world we live in. One major goal of the liberal arts is to preserve through study those things *whatsoever* that deserve to be preserved.

This conservation of what is honorable and excellent is an especially challenging task in our time due to two dominant cultural factors. The first is the constant war for our attention. Advertising, especially as manifested through social media, parades before us a constant stream of quickly fading images and messages that compete for our focus. We have endless channels on television, millions of videos on YouTube, and no end of ways to amuse ourselves. It is very hard to find amid all this noise and confusion those things of truly lasting value. A liberal arts education serves to introduce us to things that our culture has valued over time. These things—books, paintings, historical narratives, ideas, musical compositions, scientific theories, and much more—have proven their value by the persistent attention given to them over many years. For instance, any liberal arts education will include some reading in the ancient Greek epics composed by the writer known as Homer. A worldly, utilitarian view of education would dismiss these ancient books as irrelevant to today's world, but in a Christian liberal arts college we recognize that if there is something in these books that has spoken to generation after generation in an ever-changing world then we would be fools to ignore them. That is, we acknowledge that there is something commendable, something excellent in Homer's work even though he was not in possession of the full truth revealed in Christ. Because of this excellence, this commendableness, we in some sense owe these great works our attention. But how do we find Homer's epics or Bach's compositions, or John Adams's political thought amid all the noise and distractions of our age? Where do we turn amid the daily barrage of what is flimsy, what is temporary, what is shallow to find whatever is honorable and whatever is excellent? We turn to the church and to its partner the Christian liberal arts college. A primary purpose of a liberal arts education is to point us in the direction of that which is worth our attention.

But an even bigger challenge to dwelling on whatever is excellent may be the prevalence in our time of the attitude that says nothing is of any more value than anything else. This idea is often associated with the collection of philosophical and cultural views collectively known as *postmodernism*. Postmodernism is not one coherent philosophical system but rather a loose conglomeration of ideas. Nevertheless, we can identify some of its chief themes, and perhaps the biggest attribute of postmodernism is a commitment to *relativism*, the belief that truth is not a universal and unchanging thing but is, rather, determined by the individual. One simple way to think about this is that postmodernism attempts to take the capital T out of *Truth* and replace it with a bunch of lowercase "truths."

The influence of postmodernism is widespread in our culture, and, while most Christians who remain faithful to the authority of the Bible and the historical witness of the Christian church reject its demotion of truth to the level of individual experience, we are often so steeped in the postmodern attitudes around us that we don't realize how they have affected us. Rejecting postmodernist relativism means affirming that things like the laws of gravity and the rules of arithmetic are not *subjective*—not based on individual experience and perception—but rather *objective*, true for all people at all times. Further, rejecting postmodernist relativism means that the Christian affirms that there is also an objective, a universal and unchanging, foundation for morality. But Paul calls us to understand that excellence and honorableness are also objective qualities. He takes it as given that some things are, as he says, "worthy" of praise, and that must mean that some things are not. The superficial, ephemeral distractions of the moment are not to be pondered with the same reverence and respect as what is lasting. Mozart, valued for over two hundred years, is more deserving of our attention than Metallica. If Metallica is cherished two hundred years from now, we will reconsider that, I suppose, but often it is not so hard to tell the difference between the permanent things and the temporary things. Of course, that does not mean that the less permanent things are without value entirely. I like being entertained. I like pop music. I would not, however, put most television and most popular music on a level with Homer or with Beethoven. The temporary things can be pleasant and diverting, but they tend to fade when put next to the permanent things. One of the major goals of a good liberal arts education is to shape the taste of the student, which is just another way of saying to help the student think about whatever is worthy of praise. It is important to do this not out of snobbery but rather out of fidelity to the biblical truth that excellence matters.

It is very important to note that Paul also directs our attention to *whatever is lovely*. When we are considering whatever is worthy of praise and whatever is commendable, beauty matters. In the Christian life, beauty matters. An attitude that treats beauty as something extra to be attended to only after all the "real" needs are met is not a Christian attitude. In Phil 4, we are told to think about what is beautiful. A truly Christian education thus includes a substantial aesthetic element, by which I mean it necessarily values beauty in the form of art, literature, and music as well as in beautiful ideas and beautifully virtuous actions. In the Christian liberal arts tradition, poetry is valued because it is beautiful. In fact, geometry is valued also because, in its balance and harmony, it is beautiful. Paul's direction to reflect on beauty ought to cure any Christian of unconscious utilitarianism. This is not, however, because we, as is sometimes said, value "art for art's sake." Rather, we value art and all beauty as a form of testimony about God.

What Paul is pointing us toward in his letter to the Philippians may be summed up in a triad that has underpinned Christian education for centuries and to which I refer throughout this book: truth, goodness, and beauty. These three things are sometimes called the "transcendentals" because they point us beyond this world to God. They transcend the merely material world, the world we can immediately experience with our physical senses. They point us beyond our practical and utilitarian concerns to our God, who himself is the ultimate truth, the highest good, and the purest beauty. The liberal arts make these transcendentals the top priority, and in doing so they prioritize giving glory and honor to God.

This is not to say that one should abandon all practical concerns. After all, Paul himself was a tentmaker and used that craft as a means of supporting his mission and a platform for preaching the gospel. But he did not, to resort to an old cliché, "put the cart before the horse." The practical and earthly was put in service of the transcendent and eternal, and our education should follow the same pattern of priorities. Jesus tells his people to "seek first the kingdom of God" (Matt 6:33) and that the greatest commandment is to "love the Lord your God with all your heart, with all your soul, and with all your mind" (Matt 22:37). The best education is an education that helps the student do just that. A liberal arts education aims no lower than cooperating with the Holy Spirit to enable you to "be transformed by the renewing of your mind" (Rom 12:2). Such a goal is what distinguishes a truly Christian education from what is merely a secular education that happens to be provided by Christians.

2

What Is Man?

ANTHROPOLOGY 101

What is a human being? In the minds of some people, we are little more than an accident, a random accumulation of matter whittled into our current shape by the blind forces of evolution. In the minds of others, we are a unique creation of God, designed to worship him and live forever in blissful communion with him. I would suggest that there are no middle positions between these two extremes. We can't have been created *a little bit* on purpose. Life can't be a little, but not very, meaningful. We are either a purposeful creation in a meaningful cosmos, or we are the result of blind chance in a universe without purpose or meaning beyond whatever flimsy fiction we can ourselves invent. We must choose which we believe, and that choice should then determine what we believe about education.

Let me be perfectly clear: if we are the result of mere chance, then there is really not much reason to prefer a liberal education over the kind of practical education that dominates contemporary thinking about learning. In other words, most secular education makes the right choice given its assumptions about reality. If life is meaningless, it may as well be as pleasant as possible, so the kind of education that prioritizes material prosperity would be the logical choice. Education in a purposeless universe should convey only what is necessary for us to make ourselves as comfortable as possible and should require as little from us as possible. If we are accidents in a purposeless universe, then we are under no obligation to care about beauty. If life is meaningless, there is really no such thing as wisdom. In a universe without meaning, goodness is whatever we decide to prefer. Without a creator, truth might still exist as brute, unalterable fact, but we are under no obligation to care about it. Education is, in that scenario, just a means to an end.

Though one does not typically hear it articulated as such, the meaningless and materialist approach typifies much secular education today. That is to be expected. Unfortunately, many Christians also default to such materialist thinking about education. It is easy to fall into the habit of thinking an education aimed at essentially secular purposes is a "Christian" education just because chapel is required and a Bible verse is occasionally read at the beginning of class. If, however, the essential purpose of the education is secular, then no amount of Christian window-dressing will make it a Christian education. And if the purpose of the education aims only at comfort and ease, then regardless of how many chapel services are required, the underlying suggestion in and ultimate lesson from the education will be that life is meaningless, so you might as well get all the pleasure and wealth you can.

But what if life isn't meaningless? What if we are made by a creator who loves us and who gives meaning to his creation? Surely, then, life is about more than comfort and acquisition. And if human life has meaning, then something that takes up as much of our life as education ought to be about understanding that meaning, about exploring it in depth and with a sense of wonder. That is not to say that practical training is unimportant. There is a time for the kind of practical and technical instruction that leads to honest work done well. But, given the Christian understanding of what a human being is, education should not be restricted to just practical job preparation. We must prioritize wisdom, wonder, and gratitude. A Christian liberal arts education is a *humane* education not just because it involves study of the humanities but also, and primarily, because it is based on a particular understanding of what it means to be a human being.

THE *IMAGO DEI*

The Christian tradition has always affirmed that human beings are made in the image of God. The foundation for the idea of the "image of God," or *imago Dei*, is found in Gen 1:26–27.

> Then God said, "Let us make man in our image, according to our likeness. They will rule the fish of the sea, the birds of the sky, the livestock, the whole earth, and the creatures that crawl on the earth."
>
> So God created man
> in his own image;
> he created him in the image of God;
> he created them male and female.

What does it mean to say that we are made in the image of God? It obviously does not mean that we have God's infinite knowledge, wisdom, power, or goodness. One thing it does mean, however, is that we are more fully conscious than the rest of material creation. We are capable of reason, memory, and contemplation. And because of those capabilities, we are also capable of a kind of deep and rich communion with our Creator. Thus the greatest commandment is, again, to "love the Lord your God with all your heart, with all your soul, and with all your mind" (Matt 22:37). We are able, by God's grace, to fulfill this commandment because being made in God's image means we can consciously orient our hearts and minds toward him. We can choose to know and love God. God's purposes for us are closely connected with the nature of our creation.

This fact of being made in God's image must be considered the primary fact when determining what sort of education is appropriate for human beings. Our education must orient our hearts, minds, and souls toward our Creator. We achieve this orientation, of course, through learning directly about him in classes on the Bible and theology. But we also achieve it through the theologically inflected study of a full range of topics. Think back to the cake metaphor I used in the introduction to this book. When we ask questions about God's creation, we honor him as the creator. Now we can see that, in asking those questions, we are also fulfilling our place within his creation. He is the baker of the cake; we were made to eat it and to inquire into its indisputable goodness. That is our role in the order of creation. To look at the stars and marvel at their creator is part of what it means to be made in the image of God, but to ask ourselves what the stars are and to turn to the studies of men and women who have sought to answer that question is also part of living into the *imago Dei* because it is to use our reason, memory, and contemplative abilities to honor God in learning about his creation. That means that, when we take an astronomy course, we are stepping more fully into our place as human beings. Thus, Aristotle begins his *Metaphysics* by asserting that "all men by nature desire to know."[1] Aristotle did not have the benefit of Scripture to know that we are made in the image of God, but he could still discern within human nature this noble desire for knowledge and understanding.

According to Augustine—the great Christian philosopher I discussed in the introduction—learning about creation comes naturally to a creature made for the love of God. In his *Confessions*, Augustine tells the story of how he was drawn to the Christian faith by a love of wisdom and a thirst for truth. In a passage that would inspire generations of Christian educators he writes:

> And what is the object of my love? I asked the earth and it said: "It is not I." I asked all that is in it; they made the same confession (Job 28:12 f.). I asked the sea, the deeps, the living creatures that creep, and they responded: "We are not your God, look beyond us." I asked the breezes which blow and the entire air with its inhabitants said: "Anaximenes was mistaken; I am not God." I asked heaven, sun, moon and stars; they said: "Nor are we the

---

1. Aristotle, *Metaphysica* 980a21.

God whom you seek." And I said to all these things in my external environment: "Tell me of my God who you are not, tell me something about him." And with a great voice they cried out: "He made us" (Ps 99:3). My question was the attention I gave to them and their response was their beauty.[2]

Notice the breadth of Augustine's inquiry, which includes the physical world around him but also the philosophy of the ancient Greek thinker Anaximenes, which, though mistaken, is part of the search. Notice too what Augustine implies by the word *attention*. Attention is something more than a passing notice. The word implies concentration and focus and thus is something much more like study than like casual notice. Augustine is often considered one of the thinkers at the foundations of the Christian liberal arts because he shows us how prolonged and focused attention to what *is*—to all the things that exist—is a way of accessing the image of God in us in order to commune with the creator who imprinted us with that image.

To put all of that more directly, the liberal arts are important because learning is one of the things human beings have been created to do. God is omniscient, all knowing. We are not all-knowing, but as beings created in God's image, we are made to know ever more, to learn and to grow intellectually, emotionally, and spiritually.

This attribute of human beings is so obvious that it was known even to the great pagan thinkers before the time of Christ. Aristotle insisted that everything has a purpose, what he called a *telos*, and that the purpose can generally be discerned by looking at what makes the thing distinct from other things. For example, we might say that you can tell by the shape of a spoon that its purpose is to aid in eating soup, while the shape of a fork tells you that its purpose is for eating meats or vegetables. Similarly, human beings are distinguished from the rest of earthly creation by our ability to reason. It is thus reasonable to conclude that reason must be part of our *telos*, our purpose for being. From this Aristotle concludes,

2. Augustine, *Confessions*, 83.

in his *Ethics*, that the purpose of human beings is contemplation. When Christianity and its insistence on the *imago Dei* in humans is added, it is not a big step from Aristotle's conclusion to the words of the Westminster Catechism: "Man's chief end is to glorify God, and to enjoy him forever."[3] We are made for the kind of attention which Augustine gave the world so that we may hear the answer that he was given repeated again and again: "He made us."

So we learn widely, deeply, enthusiastically not just because there will be some practical, material payout for doing so but rather because it is who we are. As beings made in the image of God, learning is appropriate for us. Most people know this instinctively, even if they could not or would not articulate it directly. Does anyone really admire a couch potato? Don't we all feel that something has been wasted when we see a fellow human being choose a life of ignorance and sloth? We know deep down that we are made for more. We are part of a world, and we must give our attention to that world to honor its creator. We are also part of a human story, and we honor God as the author and chief protagonist—Christ the God-man—when we learn that story. Few endeavors in life prepare us as well for a lifetime of living into the *imago Dei* in which we are created as does a Christian liberal arts education.

It is important to acknowledge, however, that the lack of a liberal arts education certainly does not lessen the *imago Dei* in a person. The uneducated person is not less human and not less made in the image of God. Rather, we all live best in the image we have been given when we rise to honor the particular gifts we have been given. Those endowed with a capacity for advanced reason and contemplation honor God's image through reason and contemplation, while those who have those capacities in lesser amounts, or not at all, reflect the image of God in other ways: through love, creativity, and simply being, for instance. There are many ways to cultivate the *imago Dei* in all of us. For many people, a liberal arts education will be one of the most viable and extensive ways to do so, but it is not the only way, and the uneducated person, as well as the mentally handicapped person, is as much made

---

3. Pelikan and Hotchkiss, *Creeds and Confessions*, 652.

in the image of God as are the greatest scholars and thinkers of world history. What matters is how we use the abilities for thought God has given us.

If one can pursue a liberal arts education, however, one should, and this is so because we no longer live in a world in which it is possible to honor the *imago Dei* in us by remaining "a simple Christian." Earlier in the history of Western culture individual human life was shaped for most people by the yearly rhythms of agriculture, the mutual support of the family, and the constant presence of the church in daily life. In such a world, it was perhaps possible to live an authentically Christian life with little learning, leaning on the guidance of the church for one's formation. People were as sinful and misguided as ever, but most institutions shaping human life were not antithetical to the expression of the *imago Dei*. There were, of course, dehumanizing forces in the world, but they were not the major forces at work in the development of most individual lives. Most people farmed or worked at a trade, tended to family life, and followed the flow of the liturgical year. Life was often hard, of course, but they lived in a Christian world, what we might refer to historically as *Christendom*. In a later chapter, I will discuss more extensively the difference between this premodern world and the world we live in today, but, for now, I want simply to note that we no longer live in a world in which it is possible to be a "simple Christian." As C. S. Lewis, and many others, have pointed out, we live in a world today that is primarily post-Christian. In such a world, if we are not formed intentionally by robust Christian education, we will be malformed by secular culture. In premodern Europe, the church was ubiquitous, meaning it was everywhere present and influential. Today, it is pop culture which is ubiquitous, and its values and priorities will fill any void left. Thus, if we want to be shaped in a way that values the image of God innate within us, then we need the powerful counter-force of the Christian liberal arts to work against the ubiquitous shaping forces of the secular, modern world.

Another way of thinking about this matter of personal formation is that the liberal arts shape us to live more fully in the image of God in which we are made by shaping us to live *freely*. This is, after all, the original meaning of the term *liberal* arts. Remember, the word *liber* is Latin for *free*. Of course, the term as used by the ancients carried a strong bias related to what we today would call "social class." According to the ancient Greeks and Romans, the liberal arts are the arts appropriate to the free man, as opposed to the slave (or the woman). Because the slaves labored, the free man was free to think. As the idea of the liberal arts was absorbed and reshaped by Christianity, however, the definition of freedom was also slowly changed. Christianity gave to the Western world a definition of freedom not wholly dependent on the conditions of one's labor. It is important to remember that Christianity, slowly over time, helped to whittle slavery out of the heart of Western civilization precisely because Christians believe that *all* human beings are made in the image of God. If all too many individual Christians have defended that practice of slavery, in America and elsewhere, that does not change the fact that it was Christianity itself that led to the virtual extinction of slavery in the modern West.

The Christian faith, however, notes that there is more than one way to be a slave, and this is where we see the redemption of the word *liber* in the *liberal arts*. The Bible tells us that we are either free in Christ or slaves to sin (John 8:34; Gal 5:1). The Christian liberal arts aid us in living free from merely following the sinful impulses of our desires and immediate needs. They do so by introducing us to and focusing us on sources of truth, goodness, and beauty. The liberal arts also free us from a slavish dependency on the views and understandings that happen to dominate our time and place. They give us freedom to think more clearly and feel more deeply by providing us with resources beyond the brief moment of our own lifetime and context. They free us in a way that has little to do with the evil economic practice of slavery found throughout world history.

As it challenged old pagan views of human nature, Christianity brought dignity to the kind of labor once seen as *servile*, as appropriate only for those whose humanity was in some way

What Is Man?

discounted or seen as less. But in doing so, it didn't elevate two mutually exclusive options to equal but utterly distinct positions, as if one should pursue the practical arts or the liberal arts but never both. Rather, the Christian vision of the liberal arts is one of plumbers who read Augustine's *City of God* and think about the points of contrast and connection between Plato's philosophy and the Christian faith. It is a vision of lawyers who love poetry and doctors who read Roman history. The Christian liberal arts are a way of making the riches of thought and culture which were once available only to the few available to all who will apply themselves to study. Thus, the Christian liberal arts are a means of liberating human beings made in the image of God, regardless of how any one of those human beings may make his or her living.

The civil rights activist and writer W. E. B. Du Bois understood this liberating element of the liberal arts. In his famous book *The Souls of Black Folk*, he argued in opposition to those who thought that recently emancipated African-Americans could achieve true freedom simply by economic advancement. He saw a need for deep learning and cultural stewardship in the march to true equality. Du Bois emphasized both the unique contributions Americans of African descent can make to world culture and the equal share in the learned traditions of the West due to all people regardless of race. He wrote movingly of the liberal arts inheritance:

> I sit with Shakespeare and he winces not. Across the color line I move arm in arm with Balzac and Dumas, where smiling men and welcoming women glide in gilded halls. From out the caves of evening that swing between the strong-limbed earth and the tracery of the stars, I summon Aristotle and Aurelius and what soul I will, and they come all graciously with no scorn nor condescension. So, wed with Truth, I dwell above the Veil. Is this the life you grudge us, O knightly America? Is this the life you long to change into the dull red hideousness of Georgia? Are you so afraid lest peering from this high Pisgah, between Philistine and Amalekite, we sight the Promised Land?[4]

---

4. Du Bois, *Souls of Black Folk*, 102.

An Invitation to the Liberal Arts

Du Bois didn't see Aristotle, Marcus Aurelius, or Shakespeare as "dead white males" to be dismissed as irrelevant to his own experiences. He saw them as living minds to commune with through the pages of books, and in that communion he saw a key piece of his own dream of true liberty, which he speaks of metaphorically as "the Promised Land." Of course, a classical liberal arts education cannot give us salvation, not even in a Christian college. It can, however, give us the glimpse of freedom, the taste of liberty, that will compel us to keep moving toward that Promised Land.

If it is fundamental to a Christian liberal arts education to remember that all human beings are made in the image of God, it is also fundamental to remember that all human beings are sinners affected by the fall. In the seventeenth century, the great English poet and political philosopher John Milton wrote in his short book *On Education* that the true purpose of a liberal arts education is to help human beings thrive despite our fallen state:

> The end then of learning is to repair the ruins of our first parents by regaining to know God aright, and out of that knowledge to love him, to imitate him, to be like him, as we may the nearest by possessing our souls of true virtue, which being united to the heavenly grace of faith makes up the highest perfection.[5]

Milton is not suggesting that education can save us: again, only Christ can save. He is suggesting that education helps us "repair the ruins" caused by sin by restoring our reason, imagination, and affections (what we love) to something closer to the unfallen state. Thus, education is a partner in grace's work of sanctification, making us more like our savior Jesus. To participate in that work, however, we must first acknowledge our fallen and sinful state. "If we say, 'We have no sin,' we are deceiving ourselves, and the truth is not in us" (1 John 1:8).

A liberal arts education understands that sinful, fallen human beings cannot possibly discover and discern truth all by themselves, and thus good education provides resources for

---

5. Milton, *Complete Poems and Major Prose*, 631.

thinking. This includes primarily, of course, Scripture and sound commentary on the Bible. It includes also the wisdom of the ages and the chief examinations of what it means to be human. A liberal arts education should strive to include anything that may be useful on the path to wisdom, because we fallen human beings need all the help we can get. We cannot be left to "feel out" the truth on our own. Rather, we must learn to think for ourselves but never by ourselves. Understanding the limits of fallen human beings helps us understand that none of the great thinkers of the past, revere them as we may, is completely without error. But it also helps us understand that we, too, are not without error, and thus we read the great thinkers of the past broadly so that they may correct each other and fill in our own missing pieces as well. Understanding the fallen nature of humanity should encourage us not to turn away from the great conversation that is the history of thought, literature, and art but rather to enter into it understanding that Scripture itself recommends cooperation among human beings:

> Two are better than one because they have a good reward for their efforts. For if either falls, his companion can lift him up; but pity the one who falls without another to lift him up. Also, if two lie down together, they can keep warm; but how can one person alone keep warm? And if someone overpowers one person, two can resist him. A cord of three strands is not easily broken. (Eccl 4:9–12)

We think better when we think in company, and there is no reason to limit that company to the people who happen to share our time and place. We have the great luxury of helping to "repair the ruins" of the fall by thinking along with the greatest minds of the past.

The liberal arts are the most inherently Christian form of education because liberal arts education is based on a Christian understanding of human beings as created in the image of God, marred by sin, and redeemed by grace. This crucial element of the faith will inevitably shape the kind of education one seeks if one takes it seriously. It simply does not make much sense to expect good results from the kind of education that denies who we are as creatures made by God. When we approach our studies understanding that broad and deep learning is appropriate for human beings endowed with reason but also that our reason, imagination, and affections have been blunted by the fall and subsequent sin, then we are prepared to get the most good out of college.

3

Why the West?

A VERY PARTICULAR INHERITANCE

A liberal arts education traditionally focuses to a great extent on imparting the intellectual, artistic, and spiritual legacy of the Western world. There are many civilizations or cultures worth learning about as part of God's world, but, if you are reading this book, chances are Western civilization is the one you live in, regardless of your family origins. Western civilization is also, for both better and worse, the context in which we encounter the claims of the gospel, despite the origins of our faith in the East. Furthermore, due to the industrial revolution and to Western political influence, the West is the civilization most responsible for broadly shaping the globalizing modern world. A robust understanding of Western civilization is a necessary aspect of a liberal arts education for a number of reasons.

One needs to have a robust understanding of Western history in order to be a good citizen of the American republic today. The liberties enjoyed by Western Europe and America came about through a particular historical process that must be understood if it is to be maintained. It is important for citizens to understand how Western culture has fostered personal freedoms of religion, thought, and expression. The citizen who has traced the long road that leads to religious liberty will be a citizen less quick to consent to the abolition of that liberty. Yet understanding the long developmental process that resulted in our constitution and bill of rights requires significant study. Such a study begins with not only the first democracy in Athens but even further back with Hebrew ideas of innate human dignity. Such a study must take into account the ornate balancing act of the Roman constitution and the reasons for the failure of the Roman Republic. It must trace the development of English liberties from the Anglo-Saxon tribal councils to the Magna Carta to the English Civil War to the Glorious Revolution of 1688. These are all events and developments you will learn about in a good liberal arts education. To understand the philosophical texture of liberty in the Western world, one must read sources ranging from the ancient Greek historian Thucydides's account of the great Athenian leader Pericles's funeral oration for fallen Athenian soldiers to John Milton's seventeenth-century defense of free speech in his *Areopagitica*. All of this should be done before embarking on in-depth study of the establishment of the American constitution, which would include a first-hand encounter with and close reading of not just the document itself but also, at least, a few of the highlights of the Federalist Papers, which played a major role in the debate over our new form of government and are perhaps the best explanation of the reasoning behind the American constitution. Reading Locke, Montesquieu, and de Tocqueville is also highly advisable, as is acquiring a solid understanding of the excesses of the French Revolution. Such a study will require more than a throw-away "gen ed" requirement or spare elective in the midst of an otherwise thoroughly market-driven education. It will require, rather, a prolonged sojourn in the liberal arts, the very name of which is, just to remind us again, derived from the Latin word for freedom.

    Some people see in the history of the West nothing but a long series of injustices. This is a one-sided and grossly exaggerated view, but it is often based on an accurate perception of injustice in the historical record. This history of injustice is, however, far from a good reason to forsake learning about the history of the West. The injustices that have been perpetuated within Western civilization cannot be redressed without a rich historical and intellectual understanding of those injustices. Furthermore, in many cases Western civilization provides the very resources we need to correct these wrongs. Western civilization is not unique in its practice of slavery, but it is unique in how the Christian belief that human beings are made in the image of God, combined with classical precedents both for democracy and for republican representation, led to the abolition of slavery and to expanding rights for the individual. To cut off future generations from this legacy of expanding liberty is to risk diminishing the continued advance of liberty and equality for all people.

As important as the Western tradition is for our political institutions, it is perhaps even more important for our religious life. The Christian appropriation, adaptation, and absorption of ancient Greek and Roman culture led to an intellectual and artistic legacy that is one of the great spiritual resources of the church. The Western church has produced the poetry of Dante, the music of Bach, the thought of Thomas Aquinas and Martin Luther. The great Christian art and thought of the past can still draw us more richly into our own faith. It can help us think through problems in the Christian life. It can give voice to our own yearning for God. The stewardship of this legacy is a distinct responsibility of the educated Christian in the West. If these resources—from Augustine to T. S. Eliot—are to continue to contribute to the spiritual life of the church beyond the confines of a limited group of "intellectuals," then they must be taught in detail in our Christian institutions of higher learning. The great heritage of Christian creativity and thought belongs to you, but how can you claim that heritage without a significant period of study?

The Christian today must also understand the Western tradition in order to engage meaningfully and wisely with the highly secularized culture in which we now live. In order to witness effectively in a postmodern world in which many people have lost any clear sense of meaning and purpose, it is important to understand the historical, intellectual, and artistic narratives that have brought our culture to this place. How did we come to live in a "post-Christian" world? How do we not only reach out to the lost people living without meaning in that world but also reassure ourselves of meaning and purpose when we are surrounded by a culture of superficiality and nihilism and bombarded with its misguided messages about fulfillment and meaning? To do so, we need not only the rich spiritual resources mentioned above but also the sort of keen insight into the times that comes from examining modern and postmodern culture critically. A prolonged study of the Christianization and then of the secularization of the Western world provides this critical insight. Again, we study Western culture because we are still in it.

Understanding the Western tradition also serves as an inspiration in preserving the religious liberty we enjoy today in another way. A glib secular triumphalism dominates much of education at the high school and college levels. Textbooks and teachers often leave students with the impression that all things good in human history have come from the gradual shedding of the "primitive" religious beliefs that shackled the minds of our ancestors. To the minds of some modern people, the story of "progress" is the story of getting rid of religion. Is it any wonder, then, that young people don't seem particularly concerned to preserve religious liberty? If faith has contributed only to holding back the glorious progress of a world moving inexorably toward ever greater enlightenment, why worry about religious liberty? No one, however, who has read Paul's letters to the Corinthians, Dante's *Divine Comedy*, or Milton's *Paradise Lost*—rather, no one who has read them well and open-heartedly—could possibly believe that the Christian faith has contributed only oppression and grim-faced restriction to the world and not beauty, charity, and goodness. A liberal arts education creates awareness of how faith nourishes culture. Not only will students learn about the crucial role of the Christian faith in the movements to abolish slavery and to establish civil rights for all, but also they will learn how faith has partnered with reason and creativity to shape for the better the world in which we live. Christianity the oppressor and killjoy is a stereotype that can survive no real education.

So, while understanding of other civilizations is good and useful, it should be added onto a solid foundation of deep learning about the civilization we live in, rather than acquired at the expense of that knowledge. To hearken back to a metaphor I used in the introduction to this book, there are many fine houses to live in, but we have to choose one to live in or we risk dying of exposure. You can appreciate many traditions even while dwelling in one particular house. A liberal education is a way of moving in and settling down in the specific culture of the Western world.

WHAT WE MEAN WHEN WE SAY "WEST"

When we talk about "the West" we are not talking merely about geography. Western culture is defined less by boundaries on a map and more by a shared history and by closely interacting smaller cultures. These smaller cultures are by no means identical, but there are interrelated in ways that make them part of a discernible cultural family we call "the West." Spain, Australia, and the United States are all a part of the Western world, as distant as they are in location and as different as they are in culture. To talk about "Western civilization" is not to assert that medieval Ireland and modern-day France are culturally identical. Far from it. It is, rather, to see both as occupying a certain defined place in a shared history that shaped the world we live in today. The "West" is a series of connections, shared developments, and intricately intersecting storylines. My purpose here is far from to give a complete history of the Western world. My purpose, rather, is merely to point to some of the threads that bind the "West" together into a mixed but coherent tradition and to suggest why that tradition is worth knowing.

There are many places we could start when discussing the history of the West, but perhaps the best starting place is with a culture and a part of the world outside of what we normally consider the geographically western half of the globe. The people we refer to as Hebrews lived in what we today call the Middle East, but Western culture would bear little resemblance to what we know today without one strong root in the world of Moses and King David. Most significantly, these Hebrew people bring to Western culture the unique strain of monotheism, belief in one God alone, that would also give us Christianity, and without Christianity the West would be a drastically different place than it has been for the last two thousand years. We, of course, value Christianity for its truth, the salvific message of the gospel. But regardless of one's own religious beliefs, it is important to note that the monotheism begun among the Hebrews helps to shape nearly every aspect of life in the West. Our educational and intellectual traditions, our predominant notions about marriage and sexual ethics, our sense of the family and of community, the very way we count time and the rhythms of the year, and our crucial ideas about the innate dignity of all human beings, all come to us from the monotheistic faith that begins when Abraham was called to leave Ur and seek the promised land in obedience to the one true God. That is why learning about the Old Testament is important not just for those who believe it is written under the inspiration of the Holy Spirit but, rather, for everyone who lives in the context of Western institutions and traditions.

The last thing in that list in the paragraph above—innate human dignity—may very well be the most transformative idea in the history of the West. The sacred scripture of the Hebrew peoples, what we Christians call the Old Testament, offers a creation story unique in its emphasis that human beings are created "in the image of God." As we discussed in the previous chapter, this idea of the divine image in human beings, often referred to by the Latin phrase *imago Dei*, is the origin of much that is good in Western culture, including the idea of innate and inalienable human rights and of individual freedom and autonomy. This sense of the great value of the individual emerged slowly in the West in the centuries after the composition of the book of Genesis, but it eventually became a central and distinctive part of the Western understanding of religion, politics, and anthropology. There are, of course, roots for both democratic and republican forms of government in the ancient city-states of Greece and Rome. But those political organizations required the catalyst of the Judeo-Christian *imago Dei* to flower into the concept of fundamental human rights applicable to all people. In short, if there were no *imago Dei* in ancient Israel, there would very likely be no "life, liberty, and pursuit of happiness" in America.

Of course, this concept has more than just political implications. The way in which the idea of bearing God's image puts each person in a unique relationship with God influences Western psychology and shapes Western art after the rise of Christianity. To take just one example, the concept of the *imago Dei* greatly influenced the way we tell stories and over time in such a way as to lead to the creation of a unique Western form of literature: the novel. Other cultures, of course, have extended narratives in prose (as opposed to poetry), but the novel as a form that follows the interior life of a particular individual and that focuses on character development and emotional experience is a uniquely Western form. The creations of Jane Austen, Charles Dickens, Stephen King, and J. K. Rowling are unthinkable without the West's long embrace of the *imago Dei*. Our great novelists draw us into the story of the formation and development of individual souls, and we care about the development of these characters because we recognize that individual souls have value. Our stories tend to be the stories of individual souls because our concept of the *imago Dei* encourages us to think of such stories as truly important. If every person is made in God's image, then each person matters, and that is bound to affect what we produce as art, from the increasingly individualized portraits of the Renaissance to the highly personalized improvisation of jazz musicians. The faith of Abraham has deeply marked how we think about being a person.

If the Judeo-Christian heritage runs deep in Western culture, we might describe the influence of the ancient Greeks and Romans as especially wide. To start with the Greeks, just consider the number of culturally significant words that come into everyday English usage from ancient Greek: *athletics, gymnasium, philosophy, politics, democracy, geometry, astronomy, museum, music, economics*. The list goes on and on. Twenty-five-hundred years after the glory days of ancient Athens passed, it is still clear that the ancient Greeks have asserted a broad influence on our lives together in the modern world.

Western philosophy could be said to begin in Greece, first with the "pre-Socratic" philosophers and then in earnest with Plato and Aristotle, both of whom produced a kind of thought meant to shape a life, not merely to provide irrelevant intellectual exercise. These two Greeks, who lived during the latter days of the height of Athenian glory in the fifth and fourth centuries BC, set the terms for much of the Western quest for the meaning of life. Plato, who pointed us beyond the mere appearances of this world and toward a transcendent reality behind it, was not only the most important philosopher in pagan antiquity but also greatly influenced Christian thought from early in the history of the church onward. Aristotle is usually seen as a more earthly and practical philosopher than his mentor, Plato, but he too greatly influenced Christian thinking about reality, especially during the medieval period. Without these two Greek thinkers, we would not know how to even begin thinking about the nature of reality, not to mention the influence they have had on theories of politics, art, literature, public speaking, science, and countless other areas of inquiry.

After Plato and Aristotle, and after Athens had gone into decline, came a group of thinkers often referred to as the "Hellenistic" philosophers, *Hellas* being the Greek name for what we today call *Greece* and *Hellenes* what the ancient Greeks called themselves. Building on Plato and Aristotle, these philosophers outlined the various possible attitudes toward life that still form many of the options for people living today, as is apparent in the variety of names used for these philosophical groups: the stoics, the cynics, the skeptics, the epicureans. There is a good chance you use the name of one of these ancient groups of philosophers to describe your own disposition or personality all these thousands of years later. If you keep your emotions under control, you are a stoic. If you question everything, you are a skeptic. If you aim your life at the pleasures of food and good living, you are an epicurean. If you expect the worst from life, you may be a cynic. These terms we use to describe the people we encounter every day are all Greek schools of thought.

Our arts, too, would bear little resemblance to what we know today if not for the Greeks. Literature in the West begins, in a sense, with Homer and Hesiod, the names we use for the composers of the oldest epic poems in the Western world, who lived perhaps in the eighth century BC. In the fourth century BC, the great playwrights of classical Athens—Aeschylus, Sophocles, and Euripides—established expectations for theatrical performances and for what constitutes tragedy, expectations that still exert influence on theater today, as well as on other art forms, such as cinema. The Greek style of sculpture has been universally recognized as the superior style throughout most of Western history, and our statues of American statesmen, such as the Lincoln Monument, are modeled directly on the Greek approach. Perhaps most apparent in our world today is the architectural legacy of ancient Greece. Greek columns and Greek temple architecture more generally can be seen today on buildings used for government, education, church, and even banking. Start walking in almost any American neighborhood, and it shouldn't take you long to come across columns and other Greek architectural inheritances. The Greek aesthetic is with us still.

The Romans picked up the Greek traditions of thought and art and carried them forward to create masterpieces still influencing minds and souls today, such as Virgil's *Aeneid* and the *Meditations* of the philosopher emperor Marcus Aurelius. We have already discussed Rome's political heritage in the West, which lives on in Latin words we use today, such as *senate*. Rome's biggest contribution to the Western world, however, is the legacy of the Roman Empire itself. In its conquest of the world spreading out from around the Mediterranean sea, Rome brought into one conceptual unit many of the diverse peoples and cultures that would eventually form the Western world. Without the precedent of the Roman empire, it would perhaps not have been possible for later people to conceive of a unified Western world in the centuries after Christ's incarnation. We think of the West still today as a distinct cultural unit largely because the Roman empire established it as such.

This, at times very tensely, unified Roman world was the world into which Jesus Christ was born. This fact makes the history and heritage of the Romans distinctly relevant. The Roman world was the world in which the gospel arrived and began the first great period of its spread. Conditions were right for this spread, and God acted "in the fulness of time" (Gal 4:4). Out of the latter end of the Roman empire grew "Christendom," the Christian civilization that is synonymous with "the West." In fact *Christendom* may be a better term than "the West," as it is a term that would be comprehensible to most of those who have lived within it. The only reason to prefer to call it "the West" would be to more clearly include the pre-Christian roots that feed into Christendom intellectually and culturally. Still, to be clear, to speak of the West is to speak of a culture shaped by the Christian faith. The heritage you lay claim to in a liberal arts education could fairly be labeled as the heritage of Christendom. It is possible to hotly debate whether or not we in the United States are a "Christian country," but it is undebatable that we in the Western world are living in Christian, or perhaps post-Christian, civilization.

In the Middle Ages a civilization emerged in the West in which the church was the dominant cultural force and a constant part of everyday life for practically everybody living within the boundaries of the old Roman empire. The sacred/secular divide with which we live today was unknown. The philosophy, the art, the architecture, the very patterns of life that shaped the world we live in were all under the stewardship of the church. All politics was in some sense Christian politics, as all art was Christian art and all thought was Christian thought. The year was organized around Christian festivals and holy days. Every rank of society, from the feudal lord to the lowest craftsman, thought of his role in terms of his service to God. Church was not just a place to go on Sunday mornings. The church was the center of life. The Christian living today can find great resources in this heritage. We can draw on medieval Christendom to think about what a Christian civilization can be, which includes thinking about how to do politics, art, philosophy, and even agriculture in *Christianly* ways. That does not mean that the Western world was a utopia between AD 500 and 1500, but it also doesn't mean that everything "medieval" is surpassed by everything "modern." There was once a great Christian civilization in the Western world. Today's Christian would do well to take note of both its strengths and its weaknesses.

Since that world of ubiquitous faith is obviously gone now, we would also do well to understand the story of how the world we live in became secularized. We should understand the beginnings of the modern age in the Renaissance and the Reformation. We should understand how the eighteenth-century "Enlightenment," with its emphasis on practical reason and observation, shifted the way Western people think about how we know things, what is knowable, and what is worth knowing. We should understand the growing prestige of science and the shrinking influence of the church. We should understand how the horrors of the twentieth century—such as world wars, genocide, and nuclear weapons—led many into spiritual angst and nihilism, a belief in nothing. A Christian today needs to see how the world around us has become alienated from the faith that once organized all social, artistic, intellectual, and even commercial activity. How did our holy days become mere holidays? That means we need often to read books that make us uncomfortable, books by people who do not share our Christian beliefs, who are wrestling with their own dark interpretation of the world. We need to peer into the darkness in which many of our neighbors and friends are living. We need to empathize with them and understand what life without Christ looks like and feels like.

Understanding these things means not just reading *about* them but also reading *in* them. We need to let the past speak for itself through the great books of the past. That means reading works from three distinct ages in our civilization: the ancient world, Christendom, and post-Christian modernity. We need to give time and attention not just to summarizing the past but to living in it. Reading the great books is thus an important aspect of a liberal arts education, as it enables us to step into the past and consider human life from their vantage point.

Of course this tradition we are calling "the West" benefited greatly at times from cultures outside of it. We owe many good things in the West to Islam, to Africa, and to the Eastern world as well as to native traditions in America that also fall outside the mainstream of the Western tradition. To say that the West is a distinct tradition is not to assert it is an isolated or even necessarily self-sustaining tradition. We have seen that the Christian faith that has been central to Western culture comes to us from what we would call the "Eastern world." Still, despite the intertwining of West with East, it is fully possible to outline a Western tradition that can be conceptualized as the rise and fall of Christendom. How a significant part of the world became unified under a single faith and then lost that unity is a story of what the West is.

THE METAPHOR OF THE MOUNTAIN

Learning about Christendom or the Western tradition is no small undertaking. Receiving this heritage was once the whole of education in the Western world. The students of former ages received this heritage beginning from the "grammar school" in which one began to learn the grammar of the Latin language through the advanced degrees in law, medicine, and theology, all of which were based largely on readings in ancient texts. Today we often crowd this entire education into, at best, a robust core curriculum. Still, even in compact form, and even when encountered primarily in translation, it is a lot to learn. Why is it worth it?

Please allow me to add a secondary metaphor to our primary metaphors of the cake and the house. A few years ago some old friends and I began a quest to hike up as many Colorado "fourteeners" as we can. A fourteener is a mountain over fourteen thousand feet high, and there are fifty-eight of them in Colorado. These mountains aren't K2, but reaching their summits is not just a walk in the park. So why bother?

Why the West?

One reason is to show that we can do it. We began this project when the youngest of us turned forty, and part of our aim is to show that we still have the athletic endurance to complete such a strenuous hike. Likewise, you might attempt such a feat of learning—the attempt to understand the Western tradition—for the sense of accomplishment. This is not a terrible motivation. There is certainly something noble in the innate human desire to accomplish the difficult task. One good answer as to why human beings have done things like go to the moon is because we wanted to see if we could.

But there is an even better reason to climb a mountain: for the view. From the summit you can see farther. Likewise, once you've immersed yourself in the great books of the Western tradition and once you've learned about how the past shapes the present, you can see more clearly. You can stand on the summit and breathe more freely in the high mountain air because you are no longer cooped up in the small and stuffy moment. Though there are foreboding and desolate scenes within this view, there is also much that is beautiful. Some things that seemed ugly up close turn out to have great beauty when viewed from a height, and some things that seemed hugely important when you were on a level with them turn out to be entirely insignificant when you look down from the summit. It might take a good deal of effort to climb up the mountain of Christendom, but the perspective gained at the summit is well worthwhile. In fact, you may just find that you want to keep exploring and keep climbing, learning more about the West and branching out to explore other great civilizations as well.

4

The Necessary Virtues

TIME TO HIT THE GYM

If you want to grow physically stronger what can you do? You can lift weights to grow muscle. But you can't lift any weight, no matter how small, if you have no muscles at all. However under-used and atrophied your muscles may be, you will need some muscle to start lifting weights in order to grow more muscle. If you have just a little bit to start with, you can grow more through effort. This is also the relationship between virtue and education. There are some virtues you will need to possess, at least in a small amount, in order to pursue a liberal arts education, but if you pursue that education, you will likely find that you are growing stronger in these virtues. Lift a little, then a little more, and eventually you will be lifting a lot.

It has long been understood that the development of a virtuous character is an indispensable aim of higher education, and the American form of liberal arts education has historically especially emphasized this goal. The many colleges founded in our nation's early years emphasized higher education's role in shaping a virtuous citizenry for the new Republic.[1] Philosophy professor

1. Robinson, "College Founding in the New Republic," 323–41.

The Necessary Virtues

Jay Wood begins his discussion of the intellectual virtues and the liberal arts by quoting John Adams's letter to his son, in which he advises that "all the end of study is to make you a good man and a useful citizen."[2] Given the religious roots of Western education, as discussed in the second chapter of this book, this emphasis on character and virtue should not be a surprise. Indeed, even before the rise of the Christian university in the Middle Ages, learning was associated with growth in virtue by such great ancient pagan philosophers as Plato, Aristotle, and Cicero. Education in virtue, of course, begins at home and depends upon the biblical guidance of the church, but education, from kindergarten through graduate study, should provide particular ways to deepen a student's virtues.

In order for education to build our virtues, however, we must bring all the virtue we already can muster to the enterprise. We must bring our humility in order to grow more humble. We must bring our perseverance in order to grow more patient. We must bring our curiosity in order to grow more curious. We must bring our selflessness in order to grow more selfless. Bringing these qualities, we will find not only that each of these virtues is multiplied in us but also that other, arguably greater virtues are added as well. When one approaches the liberal arts with humility, patience, curiosity, and selflessness, one is also likely to grow in prudence, temperance, justice, and fortitude, the four great virtues of the classical tradition. And when one is willing to pursue such an education for the glory of God, one grows also in the great Christian virtues of faith, hope, and love. Thus, to bring virtue to the pursuit of virtue through education is truly a way of loving God with all our heart, mind, soul, and strength. A liberal arts education is not an exercise in the vapid "self-improvement" advertised by worldly educators but rather an adventure in the building of the self toward Christlikeness.

---

2. See Jay Wood, "Educating for Intellectual Character," in Davis and Ryken, *Liberal Arts for the Christian Life*, 155–65.

HUMILITY

Plato tells us a curious story about his teacher, Socrates, the man who, though he wrote nothing himself, is said to be the thinker at the root of Western philosophy as we know it. In his *Apology*, which recounts the trial of Socrates for the trumped-up charges of atheism and corrupting the youth of Athens, Plato tells the story of how the oracle at Delphi, believed to always speak the truth, proclaimed Socrates to be the wisest man in all of Greece. Thinking that this could not possibly be the case, Socrates set off on a quest to find someone wiser than himself, interviewing anyone he could find who had a reputation for wisdom. What he soon discovered is that many people who thought themselves to be wise were really no such thing, for their opinions and beliefs were generally founded on unexamined assumptions at best and utter nonsense at worst. Socrates was forced to concede that he was indeed the wisest man in Greece, since, although he professed to know nothing, he at least knew that he knew nothing. Everyone he questioned, however, seemed to be under the false impression that they knew quite a lot. As the philosopher Peter Kreeft summarizes Socrates's insight, "There are only two kinds of people, fools who think they are wise, and the wise, who know they are fools."[3] Socrates's realization is the perfect place from which to begin an education.

To put this insight in biblical terms, "The fear of the Lord is the beginning of wisdom" (Prov 9:10). We must acknowledge from the start that we are not the all-knowing God. We are fallible human beings who always have much to learn. T. S. Eliot is perhaps exaggerating for effect, but he makes his point well when he writes, "The only wisdom we can hope to acquire / Is the wisdom of humility: humility is endless."[4] Another great intellectual, A. G. Sertillanges, says that "pride is the enemy of the mind as it is of the conscience."[5] In Plato's account, Socrates interprets the oracle as meaning "this man among you, mortals, is wisest who, like Socrates, understands

---

3. Kreeft, *For Heaven's Sake*, 97.
4. Eliot, "East Coker," in *Poems of T. S. Eliot*, 188.
5. Sertillanges, *Intellectual Life*, 233.

that his wisdom is worthless."[6] When we begin our studies with this mindset—whether we are freshmen, graduate students, or the professor teaching the course for the twentieth time—then we are in the proper frame of mind to learn. If we think we have nothing to learn, we will learn nothing. If we acknowledge the limits of our understanding, then we are prepared to grow in knowledge and wisdom. Proverbs 11:2 states, "When arrogance comes, disgrace follows, / but with humility comes wisdom," and Proverbs 26:12 says, "Do you see a person who is wise in his own eyes? / There is more hope for a fool than for him." Socrates and Holy Scripture seem to concur about the inestimable value of wisdom, yet both remind us not to value our own, previously acquired wisdom more highly than that wisdom that we have not yet encountered. This applies as much to the professor as to the student. I may be further down the road of learning than are my current students, but I am on the same road. I am not innately more learned than they; I have simply been walking that road longer. It is a joy to watch them catch up with me and walk alongside me down the road toward wisdom. Arrogance can only deprive me of that joy.

Humility is particularly important when one is embarking on the study of the great books of the past. Most of the books you will encounter in a true liberal arts education have been revered for a long time. In some cases, such as the epics of Homer or the philosophy of Aristotle, these books have been read, reread, and cherished for thousands of years. Yet, it isn't always easy on the first encounter to see what is so "great" about some great books. They are demanding. They are often long and dense. They are usually about people we may not immediately see as having much in common with ourselves. They often seem at first encounter to be "irrelevant." Added to these demerits is the fact that to read old books well means shunning other, more immediate pleasures, such as television, movies, and games. Why bother?

That is where the necessity of humility comes in. We have to be willing to concede that, if we don't see something of value immediately in, say, Plato's *Republic* or Milton's *Paradise Lost*, the

---

6. Plato, *Apology*, in *Five Dialogues*, 27.

issue may not be the book but rather our own limited perspective. If a book has been considered important throughout the last several centuries, we perhaps owe it the benefit of the doubt. We thus have to be humble enough to question our first reactions when a great book doesn't immediately grab our attention. Edmund Burke, the great Anglo-Irish statesman and writer, offers us this helpful principle:

> If ever we should find ourselves disposed not to admire those writers or artists (Livy and Virgil, for instance, Raphael or Michelangelo) who all the learned had admired, not to follow our own fancies, but to study them, until we know how and what we ought to admire; and if we cannot arrive at this combination of admiration with knowledge, rather to believe that we are dull than that the rest of the world has been imposed on.[7]

In other words, when we at first don't see the value in learning about something long treasured by our culture, we have to be willing to consider that we are missing seeing something and that we should keep examining the book in question until it yields to us the same riches it has yielded to countless others.

In our natural tendency toward pride, this kind of reassessment is not usually our first reaction. More typically, we might think of "The Emperor's New Clothes," the old tale about the emperor who was tricked by clever conmen posing as tailors into thinking he was wearing clothes that were invisible only to fools. We may tell ourselves that we are the lone, brave child in the story willing to say that the emperor has no clothes. After all, there are many things in the world around us that receive much undeserving praise, many emperors with no clothes. We might be tempted to congratulate ourselves on being the one clever enough to finally see through that old fraud Virgil, or Shakespeare, or Dickens. But do we really think an emperor can go naked and undetected for one hundred, two hundred, five hundred, or a thousand years? Sure, a book can win undeserving praise for a short time, but could

---

7. Burke, "Appeal from the New to the Old Whigs," in *Works of Edmund Burke*, 212–13.

a bad book really sustain itself on the syllabi of innumerable colleges for hundreds of years without someone seeing through the ruse? Do we really think we are smarter than all the people who have traveled this road of liberal education before us? To think so is surely a monstrous act of egotism. As G. K. Chesterton, a great and greatly witty English writer, says, "Thinking in isolation and with pride ends in being an idiot. Every man who will not have softening of the heart must at last have softening of the brain."[8] The arrogance of flippantly rejecting books that have been valued for generations will lead not to a great-minded independence but rather to a perpetually childish imbecility.

If, however, we will be humble enough to concede that the great books, while by no means perfect or always right, deserve our time and attention by the very fact of their longevity in the great tradition, then we will find that the exercise of humbling ourselves to give the text in question another read will discipline us to humble ourselves in other ways as well. We will find that we are learning to seek wisdom, and truth, and goodness, and beauty beyond ourselves and beyond our own preferences. We are learning to seek goodness beyond what is easy and always at hand. We are forming a habit of humility that will enrich our lives and help us to grow in holiness.

PATIENCE

The second virtue needed for education of any kind and strengthened by a liberal arts education is patience, and it is closely related to the first virtue of humility. A person who lacks humility will find it very hard to cultivate patience. We might even say that one way to look at patience is as humility over time. It is our pride that tricks us into thinking we deserve everything we want now and that we should be able to reap the benefits of an education without the work required. When we humble ourselves, we are ready to get to the patiently pursued and patience-building life of the mind.

---

8. Chesterton, *Orthodoxy*, 37.

The unavoidable fact is that learning takes time. In the course of four years of liberal arts study, a student reads many books, some quite large. A student also conducts research and writes papers. Hopefully, students at liberal arts colleges also engage in semester-long conversations with their peers and professors about the meaning of life. All of these endeavors are easily spoiled by haste. All of these endeavors must be done with deliberate slowness and concentration. This aspect of the liberal arts is perhaps one of its most "counter-cultural" features. We live in a world of fast food, instant entertainment, and frenzied action. The liberal arts ask us to slow down, to take the time to notice, and to contemplate.

There is simply no way around it: reading great books takes time. So-called speed reading is really not reading at all. It is skimming. Since I teach at a Baptist college, I am fond of telling my students that the difference between skimming and really reading is like the difference between sprinkling and real immersion. We live in a culture of sprinkling. I'm joking about the sprinkling, but I'm serious about the superficiality of our culture. Our online culture—and sadly often our educational culture before college—encourages us to skim rather than read. We are often taught to maximize the return on our time not by making sure that we spend our time richly but by minimizing the amount of time we commit to any particular pursuit. Bright students come to college having learned to maximize their time by skimming assigned reading and relying on online study sites, such as Spark Notes, for enough information and rudimentary analysis to get them through classes and exams. But have you ever heard anyone say, "Spark Notes really changed my life"? You might get the gist of a book's contents through skimming and online notes, but you will not get its soul, and even what you get of its contents will quickly fade from memory. Shortcuts will leave you unchanged, except that you will have further reinforced in yourself the habit of making shortcuts. Your soul will not be deepened nor your mind expanded by contact with summaries and reviews. Real learning takes real engagement with real books. Superficial engagement is no substitute.

Most of the real education comes in the reading, in encountering the great minds and souls of the past in person. You cannot get it second-hand just by listening to lectures or watching videos. You need to enter into conversation with Sophocles, Jane Austen, and Søren Kierkegaard. You need to hear them out fully and think about what they say and what they see. You need repeated, slow exposure to the beauty and the wisdom in order for it to sink in. The professor is there to make the introductions and facilitate the conversation, but the books are the real teachers.

Which means many students will find upon reaching college that they must retrain their minds and bodies for patience. It should be beyond obvious to anyone paying attention that we live in an economy in which a lot of people make a lot of money by preying on our attention spans. The more they can keep us restlessly scrolling, the more ads they can put in front of us, the more money they can make. Our ability to really focus, our ability to sit in patient contemplation of a great book, has been drastically undermined, and getting that kind of patience back will require purposeful, deliberate action. We need to cultivate our attention spans.

If you want to grow in the virtue of patience and to enter fully and whole-heartedly into the liberal arts experience, I highly recommend the following steps:

1. Put the phone away when reading and in class. If your phone is visible to you, if it is nearby and accessible, some part of your mind will be waiting for it to summon you. When reading your assignments (or anything else) and when attending class, your phone should cease to exist for you. This will be hard at first, but you can do it. If you find you can't put your phone away for a few hours each day, then you should consider getting rid of it entirely.

2. Do not overschedule your out-of-class hours. Students and professors both face the temptation to fill the day with numerous enriching activities. These activities may be wonderful, but we also need to leave significant time each day

An Invitation to the Liberal Arts

for reading and quiet reflection. Extracurricular activity is an important part of the college experience, but you should not do everything. Pick a few select activities, and give yourself plenty of "downtime" for reading and contemplation. Learning is the main purpose of your time in college. It is why the college exists.

3. Take breaks while reading, but work on training your attention span to sustain longer periods of focus. Attention is a skill, and like other skills, you can improve it by practicing it.

If you can follow these steps, you will find yourself growing in the kind of patience you will need not only to read substantial books but also to work through the big questions in life, to slowly pursue answers to questions that have occupied the greatest minds in history. You are developing the kind of patience that leads to a deeper intellectual and spiritual life.

ATTENTIVENESS

Because we are fallen creatures marred by sin, humility and patience rarely come naturally to us, but our third virtue of the liberal arts, attentiveness, or curiosity, does seem to be a built-in feature of most human beings from birth onward. Just think about small children you have known. They must be slowly and patiently taught that they are not the center of the universe, a lesson that a good parent must persist in giving well into the teenage years. A small child must also be taught to patiently wait for many things. Curiosity, however, does not need to be taught. Natural curiosity is the reason parents must go to great lengths to "baby proof" their homes: covering electric outlets, securing cords on blinds, making sure cabinets are locked. Curiosity is such a powerful force in very young children that they will endanger their own lives just to see what is up with the world around them. And who hasn't been driven nearly mad by a small child's persistent questions: one "why" or "how" leading to yet another and another? One can even see this natural curiosity in the nearly obsessive hobbies of teenagers: the young man in love with baseball stats; the young woman fascinated by etymology; "choir kids," "band kids," and "drama kids" exploring their art; the budding young mechanic. Youth is an age of fascination and immersion.

Curiosity does not need to be taught, but it is sadly all too often untaught. We often have our curiosity drained out of us, if not beaten out. There are several things in our world that seem to conspire against this ingrained human curiosity. Sadly, one of those things is the way education is often gone about in our world today. Far too many schools are places of drudgery and utility rather than of curiosity and wonder. Far too many teachers have little to no idea of why anyone would actually care about the subject matter they have been entrusted to convey to their young students. They are teaching this material simply because they have been told to, because it is on the list of things to "cover" which was handed to them, either metaphorically or literally. Thus, education is treated like a tedious and meaningless task to get through before a person's "real life" can begin. Treating the acquisition of knowledge as mere drudgery is a very good way to drain away a child's natural curiosity.

Our current cultural obsession with pop culture and electronic devices also chips away at natural curiosity. We are created to seek discoveries in the world around us, in observation of nature and in the kind of learning that comes through sustained focus. Our media culture has robbed us of that focus and rewired us to seek only the easy, continuous stimulation of scrolling or mindlessly watching. We live in a world of advertising, in which attention is money, and the designers of this brave new world make a lot of money by subverting our natural curiosity into hours of scrolling through Instagram or TikTok. In her eye-opening book *Reclaiming Conversation*, sociologist, clinical psychologist, and MIT professor Sherry Turkle chronicles all the ways our addiction to personal, portable technology has drained us of social connection, focus, and curiosity. She points out that what we call "boredom" is really a spark for engaging imaginatively with the world around us:

Childhood boredom is a driver. It sparks imagination. It builds emotional resources. For the child psychoanalyst Donald W. Winnicott, a child's capacity to be bored—closely linked to the child's capacity to play contentedly alone while in the presence of a parent—is a critical sign of psychological health. Negotiating boredom is a signal developmental achievement.[9]

Curiosity is often fueled by those small moments of "boredom," moments in which we take notice of some fact or appearance and think, "I wonder why." When that disposition to wonder why dies of atrophy, real education becomes impossible. Drudgery is all that is left.

So to maintain a sense of curiosity takes effort that runs counter to the current of our contemporary world. Is it worth it? Some would say no. In fact, there is a tradition in Christianity of thinking of curiosity as a sin. One might see Eve's desire to eat the fruit and "be like God, knowing good and evil" (Gen 3:5) as a kind of curiosity. Thus, it was not uncommon to find warnings against curiosity among Christian writers in antiquity and the Middle Ages. The great authority on curiosity as a sin is Thomas Aquinas, the greatest theologian of the medieval period. Yet, Thomas is very careful to establish that the desire to know something is not in itself sinful. Rather—like any desire, be it for food or for sex or for anything else—it becomes sinful when it becomes disordered, which is to say when it is out of proportion with other goods, when it is aimed at the wrong object, or when it is pursued with wrong motivations. Thomas notes the apostle Paul's warning that "knowledge puffs up" (1 Cor 8:1), but he suggests that the problem is the pride, not the knowledge itself. When one allows oneself to grow arrogant from knowledge, then one lets a good thing lead into sin. Thomas follows Aristotle in asserting that "all men by nature desire to know," which is a good thing, but that this desire should be moderated by modesty.[10] He argues that the true end of

---

9. Turkle, *Reclaiming Conversation*, 71.
10. Thomas Aquinas, *Summa Theologica* II–II.166.2.

knowledge should be a desire to know God.[11] Thus, Thomas draws a distinction between what he calls the vice of curiosity and what he calls the virtue of *studiousness*. Curiosity might include mere nosiness about the doings of your neighbor, but studiousness is the application of your God-given desire to comprehend truth. This is a good and important distinction, and I use *curiosity* here rather than *studiousness* only because studiousness has connotations to the modern mind of the very sort of drudgery and utility away from which I want to steer our thinking about education.

The kind of curiosity or studiousness needed for and encouraged by liberal arts education is not mere nosiness and is certainly not "puffed up" arrogance but rather is a combination of attentiveness and wonder. It, too, is connected to humility, for one has to allow oneself to be captured by an idea or phenomenon to a degree at which one forgets oneself in the desire to know more. You have to be willing to let your imagination be carried away into the act of seeking knowledge. This kind of attentiveness and wonder is always on the verge of becoming prayer, or rather may really be a kind of prayer. If we can bring attentiveness and wonder to every class we take, we will find our capacity for this virtuous form of curiosity growing, and thus we will find ourselves more and more enjoying the education with which we are blessed.

SELFLESSNESS

Like the previously discussed virtues, this virtue is rooted in the virtue of humility. It may really be simply a form of applied humility. It is, however, worth discussing as a separate topic because "selflessness" is a virtue that almost entirely has been left out of our contemporary conversation about education. Think about all the advertisements you have seen for institutions of higher education. Think about all the promotional mail from colleges or all of the spots on radio or TV promoting various schools. Think about all the talk you heard from recruiters or admissions counselors when

---

11. Thomas Aquinas, *Summa Theologica* II–II.167.1.

looking into particular universities or colleges. What did they focus on? Most likely they focused entirely on what the educational experience can do for you. They likely told you about how your career prospects will be enlarged. They told you about how much fun you will have as a part of campus life. Even the more noble-minded institutions probably focused primarily on how much you will be improved. It is likely that few to none mentioned education as an obligation to others.

Are there any other spheres of life in which we encourage young Christians to engage purely for their own benefit? Do we generally make it a habit to tell young Christians that the goal of the Christian life is to serve themselves above all? Why do we teach our children on Sunday to take up their cross and follow Christ but then tell them on Monday to pursue their own desires through education? And yet, even Christian colleges tend to emphasize the benefits an education brings to the student. And, of course, there are great benefits. The colleges are not lying. They are not, however, telling the whole truth. A liberal arts education is as much a responsibility as it is a privilege, and like most great responsibilities—things like serving in the military or parenting a child—it both requires and teaches selflessness.

A liberal arts education requires the kind of selflessness that enables a person to learn things not just for the personal benefit but also because these things are worth preserving. We study certain things to preserve them for generations to come, things like the philosophical and historical processes that led to freedom of speech in the American tradition, or things like the great books. In other words, one answer to the student's question of "Why should we read the *Iliad*?" is "Because somebody has to." Perhaps in high school you read Ray Bradbury's classic novel *Fahrenheit 451*. If you haven't read this classic work of science fiction yet, I certainly hope you will. It is about a dystopian future in which reading books is a criminal activity. The novel's memorable ending—spoiler alert!—features a secret cadre of book lovers who have undertaken the great labor of memorizing a great book each, so that, for instance, one person would be responsible for being able to recite all of John

Milton's *Paradise Lost* while another person would be responsible for memorizing all of Plato's *Republic*. In that way, they hope to preserve great works of human accomplishment even when all the physical copies have been burned. In a way, all liberal arts students are part of this secret society. Not that you will be expected to memorize Dante's *Divine Comedy* in its entirety, but you will be responsible for keeping it alive so that the next generation can appreciate its beauty and wisdom. If great books are not read, they will be forgotten, and, if they are forgotten, then they are in danger of being lost entirely. The liberal arts student selflessly labors in an act of conservation. This act of conservation is an act of love not only for the beauty and wisdom of the book itself but also for future generations who should not be deprived of those riches.

If you can bring just a little selflessness to your study, you will find that virtue growing in you. This is so because to read the great books is to love them, and we naturally want to share what we love with others. You will find yourself more and more a committed conservationist of the best books and ideas of the past. Not only that, but as we are more and more exposed to the vast array of perspectives and human experiences in the past, and as we learn more about cultures and societies through time and around the world, we discover just how much bigger the world is than our own problems and concerns. When one studies deeply, one inevitably discovers that one is not the center of the universe.

THE GREAT VIRTUES

Thinkers in the Western tradition have long considered the four most important virtues to be temperance (or moderation), fortitude (courage and moral strength), justice, and prudence (or wisdom). Plato first outlined the importance of these virtues in his *Republic*, and they have been emphasized ever since by thinkers like Cicero. Christians, too, have emphasized the four cardinal virtues but have added on top of them the even greater virtues emphasized by Paul in 1 Corinthians: faith, hope, and love. The four cardinal and three theological virtues represent an ideal to strive for in improving our character and in conducting our lives.

If you will enter into your liberal arts education with the virtues of humility, patience, attentiveness, and selflessness, you will find not only that you are growing in these virtues but also that you are growing in other, perhaps even more important virtues. You will find that you are growing in the cardinal virtues of temperance, justice, fortitude, and prudence as well as in the Christian virtues of faith, hope, and love. This is so, of course, because you are encountering many good examples of these virtues in what you are reading. This is what the educational theorist David Hicks calls the "normative" function of education.[12] In our reading we form proper expectations for human life but also proper aspirations for our response to it. We learn not just who we are but also who we ought to want to be.

But you will also grow in these greater virtues simply because you have submitted yourself to be disciplined in the prerequisite virtues of humility, patience, attentiveness, and selflessness. These virtues help remove the obstacles presented by our own will and desires. When we are humbled, and focused, and patient, then we are ready to pursue justice, to practice moderation, to stand with courage, and to choose wisely. Even more importantly, we are prepared to open ourselves to the Holy Spirit's influence in our life so that we may grow in faith, hope, and love.

---

12. See Hicks, *Norms and Nobility*.

5

The Myth of the Simple Christian

THEODORE AND WILL

Wherever the Christian liberal arts are championed, you are sure to hear some seemingly pious person object that too much learning is dangerous to one's faith and that it is a far better thing to remain a "simple Christian." After all, Peter was a simple fisherman, and many of us can still call to mind humble, uneducated farmers, factory workers, and homemakers who were quiet heroes of the faith. Paul, though learned himself, says that "knowledge puffs up" (1 Cor 8:1). Why risk pride? Why risk developing doubts? Why not rest securely as a "simple Christian"? Isn't that a better route to holiness than a fancy liberal arts education?

As we discussed briefly in chapter 2, the short answer is that there is no longer any such thing as a simple Christian. We live in a world of constant input from various forms of media, a situation that creates a pervasive popular culture which shapes us in ways which we may not notice but which are profound and often profoundly unchristian. To see what I mean, consider the following two versions of a typical life, the first a typical daily rhythm for the simple person living in the Western world at practically any time from the Protestant Reformation up to the First World War and the second a typical routine for the average person in the twenty-first century. We'll call them Theodore and Will. Both are Christians.

Theodore is a Nebraska farmer in the early twentieth century. He is a young adult and not yet married, so he lives among his younger brothers and sisters on his family's farm. He wakes up early if it is summer and a little later in the colder months, depending on the natural light. The rhythms of his days are largely dependent on the changing of the seasons, giving him a sense that his life is set within a larger context of a created order and ruled by something larger than himself. He says a quick prayer and then tends to several chores around the house and farm. The season and weather, again, determine what exactly most of these chores are, reinforcing the sense that his life is shaped not by his own wishes and will but by a greater order. After his earliest chores, he will perhaps return home for a morning meal, but perhaps it is Lent and he is fasting. Much of his life is altered and shaped day by day by the liturgical calendar, the church's yearly pattern of holidays and observances. He may be fasting in preparation for Easter, or he may be anticipating a day of feasts. Either way, he is again called to conform the shape of his life to a higher reality, in this case to a reality even higher than the world of nature which shapes his waking and his chores. Since Theodore is a devout Christian in the Protestant tradition, he will spend some time after his meal reading Scripture, meditating on God's word, and praying. He is not formally educated, but his parents made sure he can read and instructed him in reading by reading Scripture with him. This time of morning devotion is brief compared to the rest of his working hours, but he will carry the words with him in his mind, as his day will not be otherwise filled with much noise or messaging. As he works his fields, he will have only the sounds of nature about him, perhaps the occasional conversation with a visiting neighbor, and his memory of his morning reading. He will break for lunch, which he will eat after offering his thanks to God for providing it.

In the evening, he will read more Scripture and perhaps pass the rest of the evening with music, storytelling, or perhaps some other instructive Christian literature, such as *The Pilgrim's Progress*.

When Sunday comes, Theodore, after several important morning chores, gathers with his local church at an early hour. They sing hymns together, actively participating in worship. The scripture is read from the pulpit, and a sermon expounds on the scripture read. Church lasts until lunch, which is then shared with family and friends. Every Sunday is like this, another way in which Theodore's life is poured into a channel not of his own making. His is a life shaped by the rhythms of nature, the liturgical calendar and weekly services, and the small and local interactions with his family and the people of his community. He is often left alone with his thoughts. Walking home from the fields as evening falls, he has nothing to do but look up at the stars as they pop out one by one in the vast Nebraska sky. This, and many similar experiences, fill him with a sense of wonder and awe. This wonder and awe lead him into quiet contemplation and intimate worship of his creator. He is a simple Christian.

Now consider his twenty-first-century counterpart. Will is a high school graduate now in his early twenties, unmarried, working a menial data-entry job, and living alone in a small apartment in Lincoln, Nebraska, in the early twenty-first century. He wakes up to the sound of his iPhone every morning at 6:00 a.m., regardless of the season, since his bedroom receives little natural light through the blinds and since he stays up most nights until after midnight watching Netflix. He lives in a world of artificial light that makes him the master of his own life rhythms. Upon waking, he lies in bed awhile, scrolling through Instagram, TikTok, or the app formerly known as Twitter, inundating his consciousness with images of competing versions of the "good life" and conflicting notions of the correct opinion on various events, all before he has even left his bed.

Full of devout intentions, Will does eventually rise from bed and sit on his couch to spend some time reading Scripture. As he, again, unlocks his phone, this time to open his Bible app, he sees a notification from one of his several social media accounts. He manages to ignore it and open the Bible app instead, but not without a lingering sense that he might be missing something important. Will has worked hard to build the discipline to set this time aside for reading Scripture, and he spends a good twenty to thirty minutes reading from the Old and New Testaments. He ends with a short prayer, rises, and turns on his television.

The morning news plays as Will goes through his morning routine of breakfast and preparing for his day. Again he is inundated with images and ideas about the good life, through advertising and lifestyle segments. There is constant talking, unceasing sound, as Will begins his day, and the holy words he so purposively sat down to read are soon lost in the general din. He pops in his earbuds and walks out the door.

Driving to work, Will listens to various podcasts: some on Christianity, some on sports, and some on pop culture. Today, he listens to a recap and analysis of a Netflix series he has been watching every night. As he travels the short stretch of interstate from his apartment to his nondescript office building downtown, he sees billboards and signs for various business, and he absorbs their messaging without even noticing.

Will spends his day in an insulated and artificially-lighted office space. His work is fairly menial and enables him to listen to podcasts throughout the day, as long as the content is not too demanding. By the end of the day, he has heard about thirty different sponsorship messages from various podcasts, each presenting a slightly different version of the thing that will make his life complete. At the end of the day, Will perhaps meets friends for dinner. Perhaps he eats alone at home. Either way, he ends his day watching Netflix or another streaming service until after midnight.

When Sunday comes, Will has his choice of quite a few churches to attend. Before he gets out of bed to go, however, he spends half an hour scrolling through social media. He chooses to drive to attend the second, later service at a large non-denominational congregation across town, because he likes the preacher and finds the large church pleasant. A greeting team meets him at the door and does their best to help him feel welcome. He finds the music deeply moving, and he feels his heart refocused on God. The sermon is very good, and he leaves the service both convicted and encouraged. When he gets in his car, his phone automatically connects and the sports podcast he was listening to on the way to church resumes. He is immediately reabsorbed into the discussion of his favorite team's playoff chances this year, after first listening to a sponsorship message from an underwear company that wryly and with a great deal of irony promises to make him more manly and attractive to women. When he gets home, he goes on Amazon to order himself a pair.

The technological world Will lives in subtly shapes him to think of himself as a little god, totally in control of his own life. He is formed by a constant stream of messages in his living environment. These messages tell him, often in deeply conflicting ways, what he ought to desire. Will is a Christian, and he tries to be a good one. But he is not a simple Christian. *Simplicity*, as such, is just not on the table.

My point is not to romanticize or glorify the past at the expense of the present. Theodore could certainly be misled by bad leadership in his local church, as many have been throughout history. Living before the modern age was certainly no path to automatic saintliness. If, however, anyone ever had a chance at being only a "simple Christian," it would be a person in the world of Theodore, not a person in the world of Will. Theodore was shaped by the rhythms of nature and the liturgy of the church. Will's life is given form by his own desires, desires enabled by technology designed to remove all limitations on what we can have and be. Yet, his life is also shaped by a constant stream of messaging that works its way into nearly every moment of his life and which manipulates those desires in ways both obvious and subtle. We aren't returning to the simple age of Theodore, unless you plan on joining the Amish. We are going to be shaped by something. The only question is by what are we going to be shaped? Will we be shaped by the noise and constant suggestions of contemporary pop culture and the news cycle, or will we be shaped by timeless wisdom grounded in a deep exploration of human nature and the human condition?

CULTURAL LITURGIES

The philosopher James K. A. Smith has spent his career exploring the ways we are shaped or formed by the culture around us and our participation in its practices and rituals. He has argued that, rather than merely decision making brains, we are embodied creatures of habit who navigate our lives based on the stories we inhabit more than by the rational decisions we make. We come to inhabit these stories by means of what Smith calls "cultural liturgies." Smith defines liturgies as "*rituals of ultimate concern*: rituals that are formative for identity, that inculcate particular visions of the good life, and do so in a way that means to trump other ritual formations."[1] In other words, a cultural liturgy is a daily, weekly, or otherwise regular act that shapes us to desire a certain way of being in the world. These liturgies might be the literal liturgies of a church service, but they might also be regular rituals like sporting events, rock concerts, or even online shopping. The habits we form and the things we aim our affection toward strongly influence who we become. Following the thought of the great Augustine, Smith asserts repeatedly that we are what we love.[2] Unless we withdraw into a remote monastery or into life with the Amish, we live in an environment in which our love is always being pulled in multiple directions. Of course, advertisements and politicians knowingly create in us desires that will lead to the results they want, whether that is purchasing a certain product or voting in a certain way. But the entertainment and art we enjoy in life also subtly shapes our desires and our perceptions about the world. Stories teach us to imagine what constitutes the good life in ways that include but go beyond our rational concepts of what is good. Something is always working to form us.

1. Smith, *Desiring the Kingdom*, 86 (emphasis original).
2. Smith, *You Are What You Love*.

The Myth of the Simple Christian

What has all this talk of formation and desire to do with the liberal arts? Quite simply, a primary purpose of Christian liberal arts education is to form the student to love what is most deserving of our love.[3] That means, of course, ultimately to love God with our whole being, mental and emotional, as Jesus tells us in Mark 12:30. Smith writes,

> The Christian university does not simply deposit ideas into mind-receptacles, thereby providing just enough education to enable credentialing for a job. No, the Christian university offers an education that is *formative*—a holistic education that not only provides knowledge but also shapes our fundamental orientation to the world.[4]

This does not mean that our education is all about feeling and not about thinking but rather that a good liberal arts education breaks down the artificial distinction between head and heart to focus on the whole person and the ways in which that person's life may be aimed toward God. A good education shapes us to love what is good and, through that love, to love the highest good, which is God.

There are many ways in which a liberal arts education can be formative of who we are. We saw in the last chapter how our virtue can be strengthened and developed through this type of education. We can now consider how this virtue formation is counter to the cultural formation that renders a "simple faith" impossible in our time and place. Whereas many of our "cultural liturgies" today train us to seek fulfillment in worldly goods and fame, the liberal arts not only exhort us to seek a higher good but they also habituate us to the contemplative pursuit of wisdom, virtue, beauty, and truth. One way to put that is that the liberal arts, over time, build in us the habit of seeking first the kingdom of God. The books you read give you varying pictures of what constitutes a good life, but the very act of reading them, and thinking about them, reinforces in you the habit of looking beyond our culture's superficial and

---

3. For a more extended discussion of this aspect of education see Sosler's excellent book *Learning to Love*.

4. Smith, *Imagining the Kingdom*, 4–5.

self-serving vision of the good life. Even when you disagree with the ultimate vision a particular book offers, you are deepened by the time spent engaging in it and you are further pulled into the search for wisdom. Even in reading philosophy or literature we disagree with, as long as the book is a good-faith effort at finding truth, we come to love wisdom more and are thus shaped for the love of heavenly wisdom. We love wisdom by seeking it, even though that search will inevitably include missteps and even dead ends. The habit of seeking wisdom forms in us more fully the love of wisdom. The habit of seeking beauty forms in us more fully the love of beauty. In today's world, absent of intentional formation of these habits through liberal arts education, we will be shaped by entertainment and public discourse to love wealth, easy fun, and our own self-created image more than we love the higher goods of truth and beauty which point us to God. Our technology will shape us to think that our whims and lowest desires are the most important things about us and that we should expect all of reality to cater to us in fulfilling those desires. Without a thorough, thoughtful, and faithful education to call us upward, we will inevitably be called downward by the fallen world we inhabit.

Consider, as just one example, how we are shaped by the movies we watch. Even if you know our Lord directs us to love others as we love ourselves, many of the movies we watch invite us to imaginatively inhabit stories in which the most important thing is the assertion of our own wishes, dreams, and identities and in which others are often merely either vehicles for or obstacles to getting what we want. Our action movies often invite us into fantasies of total self-reliance: *I'm alone against the world, and I'm kicking its ass.* Our romance movies shape us to imagine that "follow your heart" is the sure way to find the good life, regardless of the consequences for others, the inevitable disappointment such a life philosophy leads to, and the Bible's warning that "the heart is more deceitful than anything else" (Jer 17:9). Unless you shun all film and television, these stories will shape you. You will need the counter-formation of long, thoughtful study. You will need a much bigger and deeper picture of what human flourishing can look like. You will need a perspective beyond the limitations of the moment.

We must give up the idea of being a "simple Christian." Were we left alone to be shaped by natural rhythms and the purest liturgy of the church, perhaps a simple faith would be possible. Our option today, however, is not between a simple faith and a sophisticated faith but rather between a superficial cultural Christianity and a thoughtful faith strengthened by the wisdom of the ages and the pursuit of the good. Our choice is between a faith too thin to resist the powerful pull of secular cultural liturgies and a faith strengthened through the habits of contemplation and the love of truth, goodness, and beauty. These habits and loves are formed through time set aside for focused, prolonged study. Four years of liberal arts college won't, alone, guarantee such habits and love for a lifetime, but the right college education can set you on the path for a thoughtful, even contemplative, life. We must learn to love what is lovable, and, through loving the good gifts of God, we learn to love him more and most of all. Again, this is why Scripture says, "Finally, brothers, whatever is true, whatever is honorable, whatever is just, whatever is pure, whatever is lovely, whatever is commendable—if there is any moral excellence, if there is anything praiseworthy—dwell on these things" (Phil 4:8). To think about these things in the world we live in today is a counter-cultural act, and it requires a counter-cultural formation through the Christian liberal arts.

6

Leadership

LEADERSHIP STUDIES OR STUDIES FOR LEADERSHIP?

We talk a lot about leadership these days. In the last couple of decades institutes, think tanks, and seminars have all started up dedicated to developing and promoting leadership. Many colleges at least claim to evaluate potential students based on their leadership qualities and to train their students to be "tomorrow's leaders." At many schools today a student can even major in leadership or go on to obtain a graduate degree in some particular variety of leadership. Hundreds, maybe thousands, of books on leadership are published every year. The amount of podcasts on leadership seems practically infinite. We are hungry to know what leadership is and to know how to lead.

Yet, if all this discussion of leadership were effective, wouldn't we have a great abundance of fine leaders in our world today? Can you find very many people, however, who think such is the case? Has all our discussion of leadership qualities and strategies given us a society full of well-led institutions, businesses, and schools? Of course, there are moments of practical utility and maybe even of transcendent insight in all this leadership talk. The sheer amount of discussion about leadership would suggest the statistical probability that someone, somewhere, is getting some things right. But, again, few of us would say that the leaders of today are equal to the great leaders of the past. Despite our fixation on talking about leadership qualities, something seems to be lacking in contemporary leadership itself. Where are the great leaders of today to match those of the past? Perhaps it is not the study of leadership in and of itself that makes for great leaders but rather some other kind of study.

It would be an exaggeration to say that all the great leaders of the past had a liberal arts education. Clearly, many did not, including, of course, not only Jesus himself but the man who led the early church, Peter the fisherman. Still, the apostle Paul seems to have had an education a lot like what we today would call a liberal arts education; he is able to quote Greek poetry to the Athenians in his speech on Mars Hill (Acts 17) and was deeply learned in the traditions of his people. Many of our most admired leaders—like Martin Luther, George Washington, and Winston Churchill—were educated with a good foundation in the classical liberal arts and the great books of the Western tradition. When one examines the history of great leadership in the Western world, one finds that the most common factor in great leadership is some form of liberal arts education.

One can learn a lot about leadership simply from the content one is likely to read in a real liberal arts college. A future leader might read the ancient historian Plutarch, for instance, whose masterpiece is a comparison of great figures in Greek history with corresponding and contrasting figures in Roman history. In reading about the lives of Alexander the Great, Cato the Elder, and Julius Caesar, a student can learn much about what qualities make a great leader and about what to do and what not to do when one is in power. Or, to give another example, a liberal arts student may read Shakespeare's history plays and discover what personality traits, virtues, and choices caused Henry V to be remembered as the "mirror of all Christian kings," and what faults in other leaders contributed to the years of English civil strife before and after his reign. Those on a path to political leadership will of course benefit greatly from reading the theory and documents of governance in the Western world, such as the Magna Carta, the Federalist Papers, and Alexis de Tocqueville's *Democracy in America*. Why would someone intent on leading a group of people toward the future not want to avail himself or herself of the examples of great leadership in the past? Why would those who want to lead a republic not avail themselves of the opportunity to more deeply understand the history, traditions, and people of that republic?

In addition to this direct content, a potential leader will benefit greatly from the virtues imparted by a liberal arts education, which you read about in the previous two chapters of this book. Most obviously, we should desire to train up future leaders in humility, patience, attentiveness, and selflessness. When faced with complicated and monumental challenges, we want leaders whose education has shaped them neither to impatiently rush in uninformed nor hold back out of selfish cowardice. We want leaders who can focus long enough and think clearly enough to solve difficult problems, and we want leaders humble enough to know what problems they can and cannot solve. We also want leaders whose minds are not limited to the common thoughts of the moment, who have resources beyond social media and television news for thinking through a conflict or a problem. We want our leaders to be in possession of the full resources of the past. We want leaders strong in courage, temperance, justice, prudence, faith, hope, and love.

THE QUALITIES OF A GREAT LEADER

In one of the most famous philosophical meditations on the value of the liberal arts, John Henry Newman's *The Idea of a University*, the author suggests that the primary goal of a liberal arts education is to shape a student into a "gentleman." Newman's masterpiece on education was written in Great Britain in the nineteenth century. In a far more democratic time and place, we are likely to bristle at the aristocratic associations of a word like "gentleman." What

Newman seems to have meant by the term, however, could easily be thought of in terms of leadership rather than in terms of hereditary aristocracy. Newman argues that a good education gives a person "a clear conscious view of his own opinions and judgements, a truth in developing them, an eloquence in expressing them, and a force in urging them." He adds:

> It teaches him to see things as they are, to go right to the point, to disentangle a skein of thought, to detect what is sophistical, and to discard what is irrelevant. It prepares him to fill any post with credit, and to master any subject with facility. It shows him how to accommodate himself to others, how to throw himself into their state of mind, how to bring before them his own, how to influence them, how to come to an understanding with them, how to bear with them. He is at home in any society, he has common ground with every class; he knows when to speak and when to be silent; he is able to converse, he is able to listen; he can ask a question pertinently, and gain a lesson seasonably, when he has nothing to impart himself; he is ever ready, yet never in the way; he is a pleasant companion, and a comrade you can depend upon; he knows when to be serious and when to trifle, and he has a sure tact which enables him to trifle with gracefulness and to be serious with effect. He has the repose of a mind which lives in itself, while it lives in the world, and which has resources for its happiness at home when it cannot go abroad. He has a gift which serves him in public, and supports him in retirement, without which good fortune is but vulgar, and with which failure and disappointment have a charm.[1]

This is surely the kind of man or woman one could follow. This is surely the kind of leadership we need in our families, churches, communities, and businesses. Newman notes that it was a liberal arts education that developed and encouraged such qualities as these in great statesmen such as Edmund Burke, the great eighteenth-century British statesman who helped shape the modern

---

1. Newman, *Idea of a University*, 126.

conservative movement. Inquire into the education of people who have shaped politics, government, and statecraft in the modern world, and you will often find a liberal arts background.[2]

Consider the education of the great British prime minister Winston Churchill. It was Churchill who guided Great Britain through its "darkest hour" during the Second World War. His great speeches and firm governance can be credited with inspiring the perseverance that enabled a bombed and battered populace to hold out hope and eventually defeat the Nazis and their allies. Like many leaders of previous generations, Churchill's classical education began in the boarding schools of England. As a schoolboy, he wrote home to his parents about studying Greek, reading Euclid, and participating in a production of Aristophanes's *The Knights*.[3] Yet, rather than attending Oxford or Cambridge for a traditional college education in the liberal arts, Churchill was sent to the Royal Military College at Sandhurst, very likely due to the young Churchill's lack of impressive achievement in the classical studies of his youth.[4] Yet after graduating from Sandhurst and while deployed to India, Churchill became convinced that his previous education was not enough, and he threw himself into studying history, philosophy, and economics.[5] This rigorous self-education in the liberal arts helped Churchill build the clarity of thought and eloquence of speech that enabled him to effectively oppose fascism in Europe and to inspire the British people during the hardest days of the war. It also no doubt contributed to his winning of the Nobel Prize for Literature in 1953, on the merit of his extensive writings about history.

The liberal arts tradition helped prepare US presidents as well, from Thomas Jefferson to Calvin Coolidge to Ronald Reagan. The in-depth study of history, philosophy, and rhetoric prepares the mind for the demands of leading a nation, while the resources of beauty, truth, and goodness in a liberal arts education prepare

2. Newman, *Idea of a University*, 125.
3. Churchill, *Winston S. Churchill*, 89–93.
4. Pelling, *Winston Churchill*, 33, 37.
5. Palmer, "Curious Education."

the soul to hold up under the powerful demands of leadership. Speaking of the ideals conveyed by a classical education, David Hicks writes, "It lays claim to the student's will, capitalizing early on the student's youthful desire to grow up to be a Regulus or a Cincinnatus, a Jefferson or a Lincoln; and it promises him a wealth of inner resources independent of outward circumstance, like those the cabbage-eating farmers of the early Roman and American republics possessed."[6] Regulus and Cincinnatus were both ancient Roman heroes renowned for their integrity and for their virtuous leadership. To know what is truly good, to have the clarity of thought to pursue the best means to the best end, to value what is valuable and to reasonably evaluate circumstances in light of present conditions and past influences: these are the qualities of mind with which a liberal arts education can endow a future leader.

Thus, even as he fought off Viking invasions and dealt with other typical medieval problems, one of England's greatest kings, Alfred the Great, insisted that those helping him rule read and understand the great books. Alfred, who died in 899, united much of England in a time in which the British isles were politically fragmented and beset by hostile invaders. Yet, despite the constant demands of military matters and legal reforms, Alfred thought it worthwhile to devote substantial attention to the education of those who were to help him lead his people. One recent biography describes this devotion to learning:

> Alfred was convinced that learning to read would entice the minds of his noblemen to wander through the great works of Western literature and intoxicate them with the wisdom contained therein. Then, having drunk the heady draughts of learned philosophers, theologians, and poets, the noblemen of Wessex would apply their newly acquired wisdom as they worked in their own official capacities and would, subsequently, bring great blessings to Wessex. Like King Solomon of ancient Israel, King Alfred considered wisdom the quintessential kingly

---

6. Hicks, *Norms and Nobility*, 47.

virtue. Thus any man who aspired to a ruling office must begin by training himself in this royal skill.[7]

In a time in which literacy, much less learnedness, was far more difficult to achieve than in our own time, Alfred wanted those in authority under him to read the classic works of the Western tradition. With no printing press, much less the ease of the internet, to make the materials readily available, he insisted his noblemen read widely. Could today's leaders not benefit from imitating the priorities of Alfred and Solomon?

The effectiveness of such an education for leadership did not expire with the Middle Ages. In their book, *The Black Intellectual Tradition: Reading Freedom in Classical Literature*, Angel Adams Parham and Anika Prather illustrate the many ways that classical liberal arts education has contributed to leadership among African-Americans in their long struggle for equality. They argue that "throughout history, we find that most Black leaders who went on to become public servants had some connection with classical studies."[8] Parham and Prather illustrate how great leaders toward liberty and equality—people such as Frederick Douglass and Martin Luther King Jr.—drew on their knowledge of classical thought and expression to argue with great clarity and eloquence for the rights of oppressed people. Using a wealth of examples, they show the important role that the liberal arts have played in shaping leaders prepared to fight racism and injustice.

EVERYDAY LEADERSHIP

Winston Churchill and Martin Luther King Jr. are great examples of what qualities a liberal arts education can instill, but the real purpose of a liberal arts college is not to produce Jeffersons or Churchills, or at least not mainly that. Civilization will always need great leaders from time to time, but it needs regular leaders all the time. In other words, we need to produce not only the great

---

7. Merkle, *White Horse King*, 187.
8. Parham and Prather, *Black Intellectual Tradition*, 160.

and famous leaders who shape the world in big and obvious ways but also the local and personal leaders who shape the world in numerous smaller, more subtle ways. Thus the real goal of a liberal arts education as regards leadership is to produce leaders for all levels of life, including that most important component of stable civilization, the home.

Having spent the last thirty years of my life in the world of higher education, I have heard a lot of graduation speeches. Innumerable times I have heard distinguished speakers tell graduates about how they are all going to go out and "change the world." Most graduates, however, are not going to change the world. And that's okay. They shouldn't expect to change the world. Instead they should find a particular place to be and then be the goodness there. They should be willing to give themselves to a particular place. They shouldn't try to change the place they give themselves to, at least not until they have been there a good long while. They should just be the goodness there by doing specific and purposeful things: making art, feeding people, having real conversations, refusing to tell lies and talk glib nonsense, doing real work with dignity and compassion, cheerfully sharing what they have. That is true leadership. Thousands, or millions, of graduates living quietly somewhere, bringing truth, goodness, and beauty to the small places, is a much better outcome from a liberal arts education than is a bunch of would be "world changers" out there burning themselves out or obnoxiously cramming themselves down the world's throat trying vaguely to "have an impact on the world."

The liberal arts prepare regular people for the regular lives that contribute to the common good. The liberal arts can prepare a person to lead a small business with reason and ethics. The liberal arts can prepare a pastor to guide a congregation that is part of the church universal rather than an isolated modern social club. The liberal arts can make us thoughtful voters and thoughtful, articulate advocates within our political communities. Most importantly, the liberal arts can give us the spiritual, intellectual, and emotional resources for training up the next generation in the way it should go (Prov 22:6). With a liberal arts education, a business owner, a pastor, or a parent has more to draw from than the trendy thoughts of the moment. He or she has the resources of antiquity, Christendom, and the modern age.

In what is one of the world's oldest books on education, Plato's *Republic*, the great Greek philosopher outlines the kind of education appropriate for the leader class of his hypothetical city. Plato argues that the "philosopher king" must be educated to love what is good and to seek justice. A merely "practical" education could not prepare a person to lead well. This view of education was held by most people in the Western world up until sometime in the nineteenth century, when universities and colleges began to move toward specialization and practical training. One might look at the world around us and wonder if the general abandonment of the liberal arts has contributed in some way to a decline in leadership. Does our tendency toward utilitarian and narrow education have the effect of blunting our leadership? Ancient Roman philosophers such as Cicero and Marcus Aurelius spoke of a quality they called "greatness of soul." Some amount of this quality is necessary to lead either a nation or a family, and we should ask ourselves whether the education we are pursuing is encouraging or discouraging this greatness of soul.

7

STEM and the Liberal Arts

NOT JUST HUMANITIES

An unfortunate habit has developed in contemporary discussion of education: the habit of referring to "liberal arts degrees" when what is really meant is degrees in the humanities. Writers, reporters, TV commentators, and even many educators often use the term "liberal arts degrees" as a catch-all phrase for degrees in history, philosophy, English literature, or anything else they associate with such academic disciplines as distinct from the sciences and pre-professional majors. This frequent incorrect usage has given many people the false impression that the humanities and the liberal arts are simply interchangeable and synonymous terms.

As we have seen throughout this book, studies in the humanities are an essential part of the liberal arts. The study of ancient and modern languages, along with thorough reading in history, literature, and philosophy, has long been at the core of liberal studies, beginning in antiquity and developing through the Middle Ages and the Renaissance. The humanities, however, are not and never have been the whole of the liberal arts.

The historical extension of the liberal arts beyond the humanities is easily seen when we recall the original notion of the liberal arts as seven particular areas of study, a notion that helped shape Western education over the course of more than a thousand years. The three disciplines of the *trivium*—grammar, rhetoric, and logic—encompass much of what we mean today by "the humanities," a term originated by the Roman orator Cicero in the first century BC to designate the language-oriented side of the liberal arts. To those language-focused areas of study, however, the medieval university added four more, a *quadrivium*, which more closely aligns with our educational categories of science and math. The *quadrivium* consists of arithmetic, geometry, astronomy, and music. To the modern mind, music is, of course, the odd man out in this list, but music, with its intervals and octaves, was thought of by the ancients as a mathematical discipline. So, whereas the *trivium* concerns itself with language and the ideas contained by language, the *quadrivium* concerns itself with number and equation.

As science and mathematics occupied an important place in the historical liberal arts, so too is there an important place for these studies in our liberal arts colleges still today. Math and science, however, form part of the core in a liberal arts institution for very different reasons than the ones usually evoked to explain their presence at other kinds of colleges and universities. Proponents of scientific and mathematical study in the secular world tend to appeal entirely to the practical uses of science and math. Students in these fields go on to better our lives through innovation in everything from information technology to healthcare. They create technology that creates jobs and helps sustain and grow our economy. In short, science and math get things done.

This practicality is a good reason for so-called STEM (science, technology, engineering, and math) subjects to feature prominently at large universities devoted primarily to research and to career preparation. It is even a good reason to offer STEM majors at smaller colleges with a strong liberal arts core (see the next chapter on the liberal arts and the majors). The advancement of science, however, does not offer a good reason to require that all students at liberal arts colleges take courses such as College

Algebra or Astronomy. After all, surely we aren't hoping to make great "advances" in literature by requiring all students to read Homer and Shakespeare as part of the core curriculum. It would be absurd to expect all students in a freshman or sophomore introduction to biology or chemistry to go on to contribute to the sum of our scientific knowledge. To explain the place of "STEM" subjects in the liberal arts core, we must appeal to much less "practical," though no less real, considerations.

Our sharp division between the humanities and the sciences is a modern innovation, brought on by increased specialization in modern universities. It is said that Plato himself had the phrase "Let No One Ignorant of Geometry Enter Here" inscribed over the entrance to his academy in ancient Greece. In his masterpiece on education, *The Republic*, Plato, through the mouth of his mentor, Socrates, suggests that the study of math is the most fitting prelude to a life dedicated to pursuing the true and the good.[1] This tells us that, from very early in Western culture, the understanding of numbers was pursued not just, or even primarily, for practical results but also as part of the essential human quest to understand reality. To seek to know the nature of things is to value the truth for the sake of the truth. Plato's great legacy is the view that pursuit of truth is the highest calling in human life, and the words inscribed at the entrance to his academy suggest that he saw mathematics as an important part of that pursuit of truth. It is often pointed out that Plato's famous student, Aristotle, took a greater interest in the natural world than his master seems to have taken. Yet, surely Aristotle's inquiries into the natural world are an extension of his teacher's love of truth. Plato's most famous pupil thus not only gave us important developments in logic, metaphysics, and rhetoric but also helped to create the pursuit of science as we know it, even engaging in close observation of the animal kingdom to lead to the creation of the science of zoology. The desire to know the truth is at the root of scientific inquiry in the West.

Many great minds throughout history have been devoted to the pursuit of truth across the divide we draw between the

---

1. Plato, *Republic*, 204.

humanities and the STEM subjects. In twelfth-century Germany, Hildegard of Bingen, a Benedictine abbess eventually made a saint by the Catholic church, wrote church music, mystical theology, and two impressive scientific volumes on botany and the treatment of disease. You probably know the sixteenth-century genius Nicolaus Copernicus as the original champion of the theory that the Earth revolves around the sun, but he was also a gifted translator of Greek poetry. The sixteenth-century statesman and philosopher Francis Bacon was an essayist who pondered the wisdom of the ancient writers, but he is also credited with first outlining the methods of modern scientific experimentation. In the seventeenth century, Blaise Pascal both wrote a long philosophical meditation on the Christian faith and created the field of probability theory in mathematics. He also made important contributions in fluid dynamics and invented a modern form of the syringe. Gottfried Leibniz, an eighteenth-century German philosopher, not only developed calculus—an astounding contribution to mathematics—but also wrote history and studied linguistics. In the early Romantic age of the late eighteenth and early nineteenth centuries, the great German novelist, poet, and playwright Johann Wolfgang von Goethe also did important work in the study of plants and in optics, particularly color theory. These great thinkers and discovers were not limited by the irrational sense that one must care about the pursuit of truth either through language *or* through math and science but not through both. They pursued knowledge of reality by all the means available, and the liberal arts colleges of today do well to follow their example in that.

In the medieval university, the *quadrivium* was understood as the path (or four paths) that complemented the *trivium* in leading students to truth. It was typically taken up after the study of the *trivium*, with the *quadrivium* leading to the designation "Master of Arts" after a student had earned the title "Bachelor" through a study of the *trivium*. Additionally, in the early centuries of the medieval university, a revived interest in the great ancient Greek philosopher Aristotle occurred, and as the works of Aristotle came to dominate the university curriculum in the twelfth century, they brought with them much study of the natural world. Among the works of the great philosopher read by university students were *Physics, On Animals, On the Heavens, On Generation and Corruption, Meteorology, On Sense and Sensible Things*, and also a work thought to be by Aristotle, but probably not, called *On Plants*.[2] While much of this study was thought of as falling under the category of philosophy, it brought the student deeply into reflection on topics we would today classify as STEM subjects. The educator and writer Stratford Caldecott sums up the place of the *quadrivium* in the medieval university by noting that

> the assumption of this system of education was that by learning to understand the harmonies of the cosmos, our minds would be raised toward God, in whom we could find the unity from which all the harmonies derive. ... The idea that the cosmos is built on mathematical harmonies, and that numbers themselves can be a path to God, flowed from Pythagoras and Plato down to the Middle Ages, where it influenced the cathedral builders and later the artists of the Italian Renaissance. It was also one of the essential factors in the birth of science.[3]

The *quadrivium* was more than an efficient means to a practical end. It was a form of devotion to the God who is truth and who reveals himself to us especially through Scripture but also through the "book of nature," as Rom 1:20 suggests.

In the very foundations of higher education in the Western world we see a valuing of both humanities and STEM subjects as twin paths to truth. The specialization, fragmentation, and atomization that characterize modern thought and culture have encouraged us to think we must choose between these two avenues to truth, but a real education must resist that tendency to wall off one form of knowledge and wisdom from another. The liberal arts college that includes no or only scanty science and math requirements in its core is as out of sync with the liberal arts heritage as is the college that requires no languages or no ancient literature.

2. Daly, *Medieval University*, 83.
3. Caldecott, *Beauty for Truth's Sake*, 53–54.

THE *QUADRIVIUM* IN PRACTICE

So, what science and math classes should the modern liberal arts college include in its core? Of course, the history of science and math should be covered extensively in core curriculum. How else is the modern student to appreciate and understand how these pursuits have contributed to humanity's quest for knowledge over the history of the Western world? Additionally, the modern liberal arts students should, at a minimum, be exposed to and trained in the basics of at least two distinct forms of scientific inquiry. It is important for the student to be exposed to more than one science so that the student can begin to develop an understanding of the scientific endeavor itself, beyond the requirements and procedures of a particular scientific discipline. Every student at a liberal arts institution should experience for himself or herself what disciplines such as biology, chemistry, and astronomy can tell us about ourselves and about the world in which we live. These courses should be tailored for the non-specialist, in the same way that core courses in ancient epic should not assume every student is bound for a career as a classics professor. Science courses in the core curriculum should focus on helping all students understand how science pursues truth and on equipping all college graduates to make reasonable judgments on broad truth claims in the sciences. We could, using the currently conventional language of education, call this "scientific literacy."

Math requirements should serve much the same purpose as science requirements. That means that the goal of the liberal arts core math course should reach beyond making sure students can balance their checkbooks or do their taxes. The aim should be to induct students into mathematics as an avenue to truth. Thus, "basic math" will not suffice. Students should, rather, be required to engage with math at least at the level of college algebra, and preferably they would engage with the pursuit of truth through math at an even higher level. It would be fitting to require geometry as well, as would no doubt please Plato. As in science, the math requirements should lead students to appreciate mathematical knowledge as insight into the fabric of reality. They should come to appreciate math not just because it is useful but also, and more so, because it is true.

The college that requires more than the minimum of math and science is sure to meet resistance from many students, since, despite all our emphasis in K–12 education on STEM subjects, students coming out of most of our contemporary high schools seem even more unprepared for college-level work in math and science than they are for serious reading in the classics. Such lack of preparation, however, is no excuse for liberal arts colleges to abandon their responsibility to the truth. Nor is it a good reason to deprive students of the beauty inherent in mathematical order and in the wonders of physical reality. The path of knowledge is never easy, but, with the proper encouragement, students can be helped to see the rewards of a full pursuit of truth, goodness, and beauty in both the humanities and in the STEM subjects. This is the way of the liberal arts.

8

The Liberal Arts and the Major

MAJORING IN MAJORS

If you are a college student, what is the question you are most often asked when you meet new people and they become aware that you are a student? Perhaps they ask you where you go to school, but they are also very likely to ask you what you are majoring in. Despite the fact that the college major is a fairly recent invention in the long history of education in the West, we have come to think of the purpose of college mainly in terms of the major and the career it prepares one for. There are good reasons for this shift to thinking of college primarily in terms of the major: the primary reason being that college education is no longer reserved for the elite who don't need to worry so much about how they will support themselves after college. As college education expanded its reach throughout the twentieth century to include people from a wide variety of economic situations, it was only natural that greater emphasis would be placed on career preparation. This expansion of education is, of course, a good thing, but it has often come at the expense of the liberal arts. As we have more and more thought of education in terms of majors and careers, we have whittled away the liberal arts that were once the core focus of college learning. We have created a "zero sum game" mentality in which we can have either a robust liberal arts core or strong majors that prepare students to earn a living. But it need not be this way. The liberal arts and the majors can and should work together in a common goal of preparing students for all of life.

While the majors as we know them developed relatively recently, liberal arts education has served to prepare students for specific careers ever since its formational period in the Middle Ages. In the medieval university, students studied the *trivium* and the *quadrivium* with the understanding that the best students would go on to study one of three professions: medicine, law, or theology. Indeed, different colleges throughout Europe often developed reputations for and specializations in one of the three educated professions of the time. These specializations could even affect the undergraduate curriculum, as, for instance, the University of Paris came to emphasize the study of logic as a preparation for rigorous studies in theology while the medieval University of Bologna focused on the study of rhetoric in preparation for what we would today call "law school."[1]

Most Western universities no longer reserve professional preparation for after the bachelor's degree, but the liberal arts and career preparation are still best understood as partners rather than as adversaries. Some majors are, of course, extensions of certain parts of the *trivium* or *quadrivium*. If you are majoring in literature, history, philosophy, physics, or math, for instance, it is not hard to see how what you are doing harmonizes with the traditional liberal arts, regardless of what career path you may be planning for after graduation. Indeed, at a good school these disciplines will intersect in ways that echo the traditional unity of the liberal arts. For instance, if you are studying politics well, then you are reading philosophy, history, and even literature. To study physics or math is also to learn logic. A good college will resist the prominent tendency in modern education to isolate the branches of knowledge

---

1. Daly, *Medieval University*, 23.

and fragment the search for wisdom into meaningless specialization. If your college has a robust and thoughtful core curriculum, then you should be able to find a number of majors that seem to flow naturally out of that curriculum, so you can achieve a nearly seamless education.

BE PREPARED FOR THE CALL

The liberal arts, however, are also an excellent companion for those majors that do not emerge historically from the *trivium* or the *quadrivium*. Such majors are generally what we would call "preprofessional" majors, such as accounting, nursing, or engineering. There are occasionally things in the liberal arts core that provide direct foundations for these majors. An accounting major can benefit from the math offering in the core, for instance. But, more importantly, what the liberal arts really have to offer these majors are, quite simply, the wisdom and virtue necessary for any human endeavor to be done with excellence and humanity.

Take nursing, for instance. What within a liberal arts core, besides basic science, might benefit a future nurse? One learns an awful lot about suffering and mortality from a good liberal arts education. To read the Bible and to read such ancient works as the *Iliad* and the *Aeneid* is to know not just abstractly but in felt detail that suffering is inevitable in human life. As it says in Job 5:7, "humans are born for trouble / as surely as sparks fly upward." The image suggests the kind of contemplation that occurs as one sits by a campfire, watching the little sparks that fly up into the night and thinking about the inevitable experience of pain and loss in human life. This kind of quiet contemplation on the topic of the common lot of human beings can only be prepared for by hours of contemplative reading on the topic. Studying the great works that address pain and loss gives us occasion to step imaginatively into the conditions that all humans share and to examine those experiences from the inside, with the thoughts and words of talented writers to guide us. The plays of Shakespeare, the novels of Dostoevsky, and the poems of T. S. Eliot all teach us what to expect from human life. As a nurse, who must daily confront suffering and death, a real understanding of the human condition may just be the difference between a total emotional breakdown and the ability to keep serving in your calling. It may also be the difference between mere routinized mechanistic work and true compassionate humane care. A nurse who has contemplated the reality of pain in human life has the perspective needed to confront that reality every day at work. He or she can see the humanity through the suffering in a way that those who have not seriously pondered the human lot cannot. After a difficult day of dealing with illness, suffering, and death, the liberally educated nurse knows what passages of scripture, literature, and philosophy bring the most consolation or commiseration. A liberal arts education adds depth to the person who does the difficult work.

For another example consider the work of the engineer. A civil engineer, for instance, designs the structures such as roads, bridges, tunnels, and municipal buildings among which we live much of our lives. Because so few of the people building these structures today are liberally educated, we find ourselves surrounded by ugly and inhuman environments. Compare not only the great bridges built in the past, such as the famous Golden Gate Bridge, but even the small and local bridges over streams and ponds of yesteryear to today's monolithic, industrial eyesores. It is obvious that much of our public works have been designed by people who have been endowed with no love of beauty or sense of the human need for elegance and charm in our surroundings. A liberal arts education encourages a student to value differently than a cold, hard, and merely "practical" person values. The person who has studied music and literature, who has learned to see beauty in mathematics and in the design of the cosmos, knows that human beings thrive best when we live in environments that feed our souls. If your goal as an engineer is not just to profit but also to do good in the world, then you will do your work better for having been educated in the liberal arts.

Both of these examples, nursing and engineering, assume that the student intending to go into these professions wants not just to do a job but to do a job well, with dignity and in a way that contributes goodness to the world. The liberal arts pair best with the majors when one keeps in mind the concept of *vocation* or "calling." We are called by God to do good in the world through the particular kind of work for which we are best suited. For the Christian, work is something more than a means to a paycheck; it is one of the primary ways God uses us to bless our neighbors. Gene Edward Veith Jr. sums up vocation in this way:

> In God's design, each person is to love his or her neighbors and to serve them with the gifts appropriate to each vocation. This means that I serve you with my talents, and you serve me with your talents. The result is a divine division of labor in which everyone is constantly giving and receiving in a vast interchange, a unity of diverse people in a social order whose substance and energy is love.[2]

The Christian isn't just working to get by or to get to the weekend. Rather, the Christian works because we are created, called, and redeemed by a sovereign and loving God.

Although humankind was cursed with the fall to earn our bread by the sweat of our brow (Gen 3:19), our redemption in Christ means also the redemption of our labor. The great English novelist and essayist Dorothy Sayers sums this matter up well:

> Work, it seemed, was a curse and a punishment; perhaps this encouraged men to feel that no blessing and no sacrament could be associated with it. Yet the whole of Christian doctrine centers round the great paradox of redemption, which asserts that the very pains and sorrows by which fallen man is encompassed can become the instruments of his salvation, if they are accepted and transmuted by love. . . . The first Adam was cursed with labor and suffering; the redemption of labor and suffering is the triumph of the second Adam—the Carpenter nailed to the cross.[3]

---

2. Veith, *God at Work*, 40.
3. Dorothy Sayers, "Vocation in Work," in Placher, *Callings*, 405–6.

We Christians work to create because our God is a creator, and we work to redeem because our God is our redeemer. As we are new creations in Christ, our work today is more like the work given before the fall to Adam and Eve in the garden, even if we must persist in this work amid the difficult conditions of a fallen world. As Sayers points out, Adam was given the work of naming the animals, and God gave both Adam and Eve the work of tending the garden. If, then, we are participating in the building of the kingdom of God when we build tunnels, or paint houses, or argue court cases, then we want to do these things with more than perfunctory technical accuracy. We need a kind of education that prepares us to work not just with our hands or even just with our minds but also with our hearts and souls. In this way, the liberal arts institution takes the major not less but rather more seriously than the purely "technical" or utterly "career-oriented" educational establishment. From the perspective of the Christian liberal arts, every true calling—every form of honest work—is a high calling that should be pursued with an enriched mind and soul.

PEOPLE OF LEISURE

But our work, whether it is as an airplane pilot or a kindergarten teacher, is only one important part of who we are. Thus, the liberal arts pair well with any major also because the liberal arts nourish parts of our humanity that our work may not necessarily nourish. After all, Jesus teaches us both how to ask for our daily bread (Matt 6:11) *and* that "man must not live on bread alone" (Matt 4:4). He means, of course, that we need God and his word, and, because we are spiritual beings, we need nourishment of our souls. Human beings need beauty, and we need to ponder, to think about things. Put quite simply, a good liberal arts education prepares you for your leisure hours. That does not, however, put the liberal arts part of your education at odds with your education in a particular major. Rather, it means that the two components of your education are complementary.

Our culture today has a very debased sense of leisure. We associate relaxation with a lack of thought, even likening ourselves at times to "vegetables" in our state of relaxation. This has not always been the case. Among the ancient Greeks and Romans, leisure was thought of differently than how we think about it today. The ancients saw in leisure time the opportunity for ennobling activity such as reading and study. One scholar of classics, Michael O'Loughlin, describes the ancient view of leisure this way: "The Greeks had a word for it: *schoolē*. Their word for leisure is the root of our word 'school.' What they had in mind as 'free' time survives in what we still appropriately call the 'liberal arts.'"[4] Few students today would think of their hours in school as hours of leisure. Yet, among the ancients, reading and reflecting on life were seen as the essence of relaxation. That, of course, does not mean that they made no time for games, feasts, and other forms of relaxation. Such leisure activities are also part of what it is to be human. But the ancients never associated leisure with cultivating inactivity of mind, as if we refresh ourselves by making ourselves more stupid. The great Roman statesman and orator Cicero often expressed a wish to escape from the duties of public life and devote himself to the pursuit of wisdom as a form of leisure. How much more should the Christian, then, value a leisure that is ennobling and nourishing over the false leisure of our world today, which will often leave one disappointed, empty, and more tired than when one began. We should consider, once again, the words of Phil 4:8: "Finally brothers and sisters, whatever is true, whatever is honorable, whatever is just, whatever is pure, whatever is lovely, whatever is commendable—if there is any moral excellence and if there is anything praiseworthy—dwell on these things." Again, we are right that we should take this verse as direction to avoid filthy forms of entertainment. But notice again that the direction here is not in the negative. It does not tell us what *not* to think about but rather what we *should* focus on. What if we took this verse as a guiding principle for our leisure hours? How might we then best prepare ourselves to meet this high standard of noble

---

4. O'Loughlin, *Garlands of Repose*, 5–6.

and ennobling leisure? How would our entertainment and our downtime change if we applied this verse to our leisure?

That is where your liberal arts education comes in. A true liberal arts education points students toward those things most worthy of their time and attention during their leisure hours. The liberal arts student learns to appreciate good music, which means that a student in a liberal arts college does not take a music class just to have the subject "covered" or "mastered" so that he or she can move on to other subjects. Rather, the liberal arts student takes a course in music in order to be initiated into a lifetime habit of listening to quality music. The same is obviously true in courses on art and literature, but it is true, too, for courses in history and science. All classes should leave you with the strong impression that seeking truth is a pleasant and good way to spend your free time, and your classes should leave you also with the inclination to do just that.

Thus, it is okay that no course can possibly "cover" its subject. When I teach a course on, for instance, ancient Roman literature, I know that not only will we be unable to read for class every interesting and worthy work of Roman literature but also that we will not have nearly enough time in class to fully explore every relevant and interesting aspect of the works of literature we do read. My responsibility cannot be to "cover" the topic. My responsibility is to get the students started on a lifelong journey. A good liberal arts education should leave you not with the feeling of having completed a topic but rather with the strong sensation of having properly begun it. A class now is fuel for leisure hours for years to come.

This emphasis on leisure perhaps sounds strange to you, and that is because thinking of leisure time as nothing more than a self-indulgent "downtime" before being forced back into work is a deeply ingrained habit of thought in the modern world. Never before in history has a people so craved leisure and yet endowed it with so little value. This is also a thoroughly secular habit of thought in as much as it assumes we are merely physical beings. In the liberal arts tradition, the balanced goal of equipping you for your calling and ennobling your leisure hours grows from the foundational assumption that you have a soul and that you are made in the image of God. An education that cares only for your future "productivity" is an education that sees you only as a useful tool in a large machine of economic "progress." There is no reason for education to take such a view, and it has been only in the last hundred or so years, under the influence of an increasingly secular culture, that education has taken such a reductive view of the human being. The liberal arts are Christian at their core because they assume that each human being is made in the image of God and thus is responsive to truth, goodness, and beauty both when at work and when at rest.

So one important aspect of the liberal arts is to shape your tastes. As unpopular as it may be to say so in our thoroughly egalitarian society, there are things more worthy of our leisurely attention than others. There are, in the words of Paul to the Philippians, things that are *excellent*. A liberal arts education ought to point these things out to you, making the introductions so that you can form a lasting relationship with Beethoven or Shakespeare or the thousands of species of butterflies in God's world. In our sinful complacency, we would like to be left with the tastes we entered with, but we should allow education to call us upward to better things. In 1 Cor 3:2, Paul uses a baby's diet of milk as an analogy for the difference between elementary starting places in the faith and the real nourishment of spiritual growth. Most babies, of course, would be content to stick with the milk were they not introduced to better fare. We, too, need to be introduced to the more nourishing forms of thought and beauty so that we can leave behind our childish foods. Many in our culture today, going through the typical forms of secular education, never have their taste for higher things awakened, and, thus, while they may perform an economic function adequately, they remain spiritual and mental children their whole lives. A good liberal arts education prepares you to do your work like an adult but also not to regress to infancy in your leisure hours.

So, a student's course of study in the liberal arts must be balanced between courses specifically within a major and courses that are part of a "core" education. Beware of colleges and universities with little to no core requirements. Those schools are openly telling you that they see no value in the things shared by all human beings. Those schools are directly telling you that they think of you as nothing more than your economic function. Beware, also, of schools that claim to value "the liberal arts" but only as a set of specific majors, such as philosophy, literature, or history. If a college doesn't think you should know at least a little something about mathematics, then that school doesn't believe you are created in the image of the God of truth.

I would like to end this chapter, the last main chapter of the book, with a personal confession: I don't really care all that much what my students end up doing for a living. Please don't take that the wrong way. I wish them well. In fact, I do more than wish it; I pray they will flourish. I pray they will find good and meaningful work to do in the world and will live lives of service in a particular place. I also pray they will be able to support themselves and their families. I do not, however, have the slightest interest in seeing them "get ahead in life." Nor am I interested in seeing them "succeed," at least not in the way we usually define "success" today. I want them to be virtuous and wise. It makes little difference to me if they are virtuous and wise lawyers or virtuous and wise plumbers, though I do pray they will hear God's particular calling for them.

Whatever my students end up doing, whatever career or careers may occupy them in the future, I pray that they will serve others and do their work with integrity and humanity. My "indifference" to their future careers is not born out of a disrespect for the various majors and career paths. On the contrary, it is born out of a sense that all legitimate occupations are equally worthy of respect. It is born out of the conviction that any honest work done well can be honoring to God. Certainly, I do not hope for them all to become English professors or teachers of the great books. Rather, my prayer is that my work teaching in a liberal arts college will contribute to generations of doctors who read the *Aeneid*, mechanics who contemplate Plato's ideal republic, and homemakers who can recite the poems of William Wordsworth. Our liberal arts colleges ought to produce graduates who teach kindergarten and love the beauty of advanced geometry. Our liberal arts colleges ought to produce farmers who read medieval tales of King Arthur after a hard day's work in the fields and CEOs of major corporations who are still thinking their way through the historical range of positions on the question of free will. This is how the liberal arts and vocational education complement one another, by building a whole and flourishing life of contemplation and of service.

Conclusion
The Liberal Arts in Our Time

Live in the moment. I would wager you have heard this bit of advice many times already in your life. If we hear this advice as a call to attentiveness, a call to be aware of the world around us and present for the people in our lives, then it is, indeed, good advice. If, however, the person who tells us to *live in the moment* is advising us to live heedless of the past and the future and to think about only the desires and demands of the present moment, then, hopefully, this book has shown you the foolishness of such advice. Deciding to *live in the moment* is like deciding to live in your bathroom when you have a whole house you could occupy. Like most residential bathrooms, the moment is relatively small. To live well, we need to spread out in the whole house of our inheritance. To live in a way that allows us to flourish in our inherently and uniquely human way, we need the spiritual, intellectual, political, social, and artistic resources of the past. As I have tried to show throughout this book, a liberal arts education is a way to take possession of the whole house, to live in a much roomier place than merely the moment.

Yet, I hope I have also made it clear that a liberal arts education meets the very particular needs of our times as well. In fact, it is the very power of the liberal arts to return the riches of the past to us that makes such an education so necessary at this point in time. Because we are more than ever bombarded with the message to *live in the moment*, we need the liberal arts more than ever. We live in a culture that almost always prioritizes the moment. We live in a culture of amnesia. Because it restores our deeper cultural inheritance to us, a liberal arts education is profoundly counter-cultural in our superficial age.

And who could deny that we are living in an age of superficiality? Our attention spans are shrinking at an unprecedented rate so that we are all being conformed to the image of Dory from *Finding Nemo*. We are constantly entertained, but usually in a way that caters to our lowest instincts and desires. Fewer and fewer people read books. Fewer and fewer people have real conversations. Our minds are preoccupied with celebrity gossip and twenty-second snippets of video. Even when we want to swim against this tide of superficiality, we often find it too hard to do so alone. We need the formative power of a liberal arts education to shape our affections for the true, the good, and the beautiful.

As we saw in chapter 5, it is no longer possible to remain a "simple Christian." We must, therefore, think very carefully about what kind of education we are going to pursue. There is a reason we have, for centuries, referred to the college a person graduates from as his or her *alma mater*. The Latin phrase means "nourishing mother," and it suggests that our education very much shapes who we are. After all, who plays a bigger role in shaping a person's character than his or her mother? Like a mother, a good college nourishes you. You may or may not enjoy the food in your university cafeteria, but the more important nourishment you receive in college is the nourishment of your mind and soul. A good college will send you out into the world a deeper, more thoughtful, more reasonable, and more civilized person than who you were when you were first admitted to the school. A good college will thus inevitably put you at odds with our superficial times by nourishing your mind and soul to live in the larger mansion of past, present, and future.

Although you may not realize it as you start out, this is precisely the education you long for. I can make this confident statement about your desire for real education because I know that

CONCLUSION

truth, goodness, and beauty are real human needs. As Scripture tells us, God has placed eternity in our hearts (Eccl 3:11), which means we yearn for the avenue upward and onward offered by truth, goodness, and beauty. In our age of superficiality, we are largely starved for these pathways to the eternal. I think most of us know this deep down, even if we try to bury those needs for something higher in a constant avalanche of distractions. The ugliness and superficiality that typifies the world around us leaves us disgruntled and looking for more. A liberal arts education is an opportunity to start building a life of *more*. That is to say, a liberal education is a foundation for a life spent pursuing and honoring truth, goodness, and beauty.

Thus, when you undertake a liberal arts education, you are not just doing something for yourself. You are, rather, joining a great project of cultural renewal. Imagine the difference it could make for the world if our leaders—both on the world stage and in the smallest family—were educated to pursue wisdom and grow in virtue. Imagine what it would be like if we reverenced long deceased great thinkers and writers the way we do the current crop of pop stars and movie actors. What if our architects and builders cared about restoring simple beauty to the environments we live in? What if our entertainers cared not just about attracting enough eyeballs but also, and more, about what is happening to the minds behind those eyes? This project of renewal in our culture will require some of the liberally educated to become educators themselves, and I hope some of the people reading this book will go on to become professors and teachers in K–12 schools who passionately share the love of truth, goodness, and beauty (and thus the love of God) with the next generation. Even more than that, however, cultural renewal will require the participation of "regular" people with "regular" jobs.

In chapter 8 we saw how a liberal arts education is compatible with majoring in a field you may feel called to work in, and in chapter 7 we saw that a liberal arts education extends beyond the humanities into STEM fields as well. This broad purview of liberal education is an important aspect of its role in cultural renewal. To reverse the tide of superficiality in our time, we need more than professors and teachers. We need engineers who love to read. We need scientists who have pondered the natural limits of human ability and power. We need leaders in government and industry who have embraced historical, theological, philosophical, and literary lessons about humility. We need a more thoughtful and virtuous public to maintain our classically inflected republic.

Of course, the liberally educated are only a small minority in our time. It has always been the case that those who receive a quality education are few. The difference is that, in our time, that opportunity is not reserved solely for the wealthy or the "well-born." The person of average and below average financial means has ample opportunity today for a quality education, if you know where to look for it. Anyone can join the effort for cultural renewal, and, while the number of the well-educated has always been small, that small number has also always had an outsized influence on our culture. That can be the case again today, if we pursue liberal arts education and cultural renewal with a fresh sense of intentionality.

So what should you do?

If you are a high school student thinking about where to go to college, choose carefully. Before you enroll anywhere, ask them about the core curriculum. You can, of course, take many valuable classes at colleges where those classes are not required, but what a college requires in the core is a good sign of what a college really values. You can take courses in the *trivium* and *quadrivium* at most universities, but you probably should not take them at a college that does not think such studies are really important. So, it is best to avoid institutions that either don't have a core curriculum or that have a core that has been watered down to nothing more than a smattering of cafeteria-style "distribution" credits. Look for a school that has the courage to put some conviction into its requirements. Try to find out what they consider to be essential in an education. Go ahead and ask them what books you are likely to read in your time studying with them.

Also, pay attention to the way a school courts you during your phase of visiting and exploring your college options. What are the

Conclusion

college's advertising campaigns and promotional materials like? Do they talk only about all the economic and social benefits you will get from attending their school? Do they talk only about what they can do for you? Or do they cast a more profound vision for education? Look for a school that is calling you up to something higher than self-fulfillment or career "success." Look for the school that invites you to be part of something larger than yourself. They are rare, but schools with vision—true liberal arts colleges worthy of the name—are still out there.

But what if you have already chosen your college and you have, either by design or by accident, managed to enroll in one of the rare true liberal arts institutions? If you are a student newly enrolled in a liberal arts college, then it is important that you begin right from the start to cultivate the right disposition and virtues for study. You may or may not have picked up some bad habits in high school. You might, for instance, have attended a high school in which it was possible to fake your way through most reading assignments, by skimming and looking up summaries online. Expecting to grow intellectually and spiritually by skimming and reading summaries is like going to the gym and expecting to grow muscle by watching other people exercise. If you have slid by in the past, it is time to take up responsibility for your own education in earnest. I hope this book has shown you that a liberal arts education is a noble endeavor, one that deserves your serious effort. I also hope it has shown you the delights of such an education that are available when a person really gives himself or herself over to the adventure of learning.

If you are embarking on a liberal arts education, try to do so with a spirit of adventure and excitement. Students often ask me what they can do to make sure their grades are satisfactory, but, if you make it your aim to learn everything you can, your grades will take care of themselves. If your desire is to truly inhabit the house of your inheritance and to truly enjoy the cake of creation, you will be able to study joyfully, without keeping one eye constantly on the gradebook.

An Invitation to the Liberal Arts

Whoever you are, you will find that liberal learning is a high calling, a noble endeavor that will ask a lot of you. A true liberal arts education is an act of worship and a claiming of an inheritance. A liberal arts education is the most intentional and direct way to dwell on those things that are true, lovely, excellent, and noble (Phil 4:8). Move into the house. Sit down with the baker.

You will not regret it.

Bibliography

Aristotle. *Metaphysica*. Edited by W. D. Ross. Vol. 8 of *The Works of Aristotle Translated into English*. Oxford: Clarendon, 1940.
Augustine. *Confessions*. Translated by Henry Chadwick. Oxford: Oxford University Press, 1992.
Burke, Edmund. *The Works of Edmund Burke*. Vol. 4. Boston: Little, Brown, 1901.
Caldecott, Stratford. *Beauty for Truth's Sake: On the Re-Enchantment of Education*. Grand Rapids: Brazos, 2009.
Chesterton, G. K. *Orthodoxy*. Peabody, MA: Hendrickson, 2006.
Churchill, Randolph S. *Winston S. Churchill: Youth, 1874–1900*. Boston: Houghton Mifflin, 1966.
Daly, Lowrie J. *The Medieval University: 1200–1400*. New York: Sheed and Ward, 1961.
Davis, Jeffry C., and Philip G. Ryken, eds. *Liberal Arts for the Christian Life*. Wheaton, IL: Crossway, 2012.
Du Bois, W. E. B. *The Souls of Black Folk*. Edited by David W. Blight and Robert Gooding-Williams. Boston: Bedford, 1997.
Eliot, T. S. *The Poems of T. S. Eliot*. Vol. 1. Edited by Christopher Ricks and Jim McCue. Baltimore: Johns Hopkins University Press, 2015.
Hicks, David. *Norms and Nobility: A Treatise on Education*. New York: Praeger, 1981.
Kreeft, Peter. *For Heaven's Sake: The Rewards of the Virtuous Life*. Nashville: Thomas Nelson, 1986.
Merkle, Benjamin. *The White Horse King: The Life of Alfred the Great*. Nashville: Thomas Nelson, 2009.
Milton, John. *Complete Poems and Major Prose*. Edited by Merritt Y. Hughes. Indianapolis: Hackett, 2003.
Newman, John Henry. *The Idea of a University*. London: Aeterna, 2015.
O'Loughlin, Michael. *The Garlands of Repose: Literary Celebrations of Civic and Retired Leisure*. Chicago: University of Chicago Press, 1978.

Bibliography

Palmer, Zachary. "A Curious Education: Winston Churchill and the Teaching of a Statesman." *Imaginative Conservative*, June 17, 2020. https://theimaginativeconservative.org/2020/06/curious-education-winston-churchill-zachary-palmer.html.

Parham, Angel Adams, and Anika Prather. *The Black Intellectual Tradition: Reading Freedom in Classical Literature*. Camp Hill, PA: Classical Academic, 2022.

Pelikan, Jaroslav, and Valerie Hotchkiss, eds. *Creeds and Confessions of the Reformation Era*. Vol. 2.4 of *Creed and Confessions of Faith in the Christian Tradition*. New Haven, CT: Yale University Press, 2003.

Pelling, Henry. *Winston Churchill*. New York: E. P. Dutton, 1974.

Placher, William C., ed. *Callings: Twenty Centuries of Christian Wisdom on Vocation*. Grand Rapids: Eerdmans, 2005.

Plato. *Five Dialogues: Euthyphro, Apology, Crito, Meno, Phaedo*. Translated by G. M. A. Grube and John M. Cooper. 2nd ed. Indianapolis: Hackett, 2002.

———. *The Republic*. Translated by Alan Bloom. New York: Basic, 2016.

Robinson, David. "College Founding in the New Republic, 1776–1800." *History of Education Quarterly* 23 (1983) 323–41.

Sertillanges, A. G. *The Intellectual Life: Its Spirit, Conditions, Methods*. Translated by Mary Ryan. Washington, DC: Catholic University of America Press, 1987.

Smith, James K. A. *Desiring the Kingdom: Worship, Worldview, and Cultural Formation*. Grand Rapids: Baker Academic, 2009.

———. *Imagining the Kingdom: How Worship Works*. Grand Rapids: Baker Academic, 2013.

———. *You Are What You Love: The Spiritual Power of Habit*. Grand Rapids: Brazos, 2016.

Sosler, Alex. *Learning to Love: Christian Higher Education as Pilgrimage*. Beaver Falls, PA: Falls City, 2023.

Thomas Aquinas. *Summa Theologica: Complete English Edition in Five Volumes*. Translated by Fathers of the English Dominican Province. Vol. 4. Notre Dame, IN: Ave Maria, 1948.

Turkle, Sherry. *Reclaiming Conversation: The Power of Talk in a Digital Age*. New York: Penguin, 2015.

Veith, Edward Gene, Jr. *God at Work*. Wheaton, IL: Crossway, 2011.

Waltke, Bruce K. *The Book of Proverbs, Chapters 1–15*. New International Commentary on the Old Testament. Grand Rapids: Eerdmans, 2004.

The Yale Corporation. *Charter and Legislation*. New Haven, CT: Yale University, 1976. https://www.yale.edu/sites/default/files/files/University-Charter.pdf.

Subject Index

Abraham, 41
Accounting, 90
Adams, John, 20, 49
Aeschylus, 43
Affections, 2, 5, 32, 96, 100
Albert the Great, 16
Alexander the Great, 73
Alfred the Great, 77–78
Algebra, 86
Anaximenes, 27
Anglo-Saxons, 36
Anthropology, 23–34, 40
Aquinas, Thomas, see Thomas Aquinas
Architecture, 43, 44, 101
Aristotle, 2, 26, 27–28, 32, 41, 49, 51, 58, 83, 84–85
Aristophanes, 76
Arthur, King of England, 98
Astronomy, 26, 82, 83, 84, 86
Athenian Democracy, 36, 37, 41
Attentiveness, 56–59, 74
Augustine, Saint, 3, 13, 26–27, 28, 31, 37, 68
Austen, Jane, 41, 55
Australia, 39

Bach, Johann Sebastian, 20, 37
Bacon, Francis, 84
Beauty, 21, 24, 61, 70, 87, 91, 93, 96, 98

Beethoven Ludwig von, 21, 96
Bible, 14, 20, 26, 33, 64, 65, 90
Bill of Rights, 36
Biology, 83, 86
Boredom, 57–58
Botany, 84
Bradbury, Ray, 60–61
Bunyon, John, 65
Burke, Edmund, 52, 75

Calculus, 84
Caldecott, Stratford, 85
Cato the Elder, 73
Chemistry, 83, 86
Chesterton, G.K., 53
Christendom, 29, 44, 46, 47, 80
Christianity, 30
Christlikeness, 49
Churchill, Winston, 73, 76, 78
Cicero, 3, 49, 61, 80, 82, 94
Cincinnatus, 77
Citizenship, 5, 13, 35–36, 48, 79, 102
Civil War, English, 36
Contemplation, 8, 25, 54, 90, 93, 98
Constitution of the United States, 36
Coolidge, Calvin, 76
Copernicus, Nicolaus, 84

Subject Index

Core curriculum, 13, 46, 82, 86, 89, 90, 97, 102
Curiosity, 49, 56–59
Cynicism, 42

Dante, 37, 38, 61
Dickens, Charles, 41, 52
Dostoevsky, Fydor, 90
Douglass, Frederick, 78
Du Bois, W.E.B., 31–32

Eliot, T.S., 19, 37, 50, 90
Engineering, 90, 91, 102
Enlightenment, 6, 45
Epicureanism, 42
Euclid, 76
Euripides, 43
Exodus, 2

Faith, 49, 62, 74
Fall of man, 32–34, 93
Federalist Papers, 36, 74
Finding Nemo, 100
Formation, 14, 68–69
Fortitude, 49, 61–62, 74
France, 39
French Revolution, 36

Geometry, 21, 83, 86, 98
Glorious Revolution, 36
Goethe, Johann Wolfgang von, 84
Golden Gate Bridge, 91
Graduation speeches, 79
Great Books, 19, 46, 51–53, 54, 60–61, 73, 90
Greatness of soul, 80
Greco-Roman Civilization, 41–44, 73, 77, 93, 94

Harvard, 12
Hebraic Civilization, 36, 40–41
Henry V, 73
Hesiod, 43
Hicks, David, 62, 77
Hildegard of Bingen, 84

History, 31
Holy Spirit, 18, 62
Homer, 19–20, 21, 43, 51, 60, 83, 90
Hope, 49, 62, 74
Humanities, 81–82, 101
Humility, 49, 50–53, 59, 74, 102

Image of God, 25–20, 37, 40–41, 96
Ireland, 39
Instagram, 57

Jazz, 41
Jefferson, Thomas, 76, 77, 78
Jerimiah, 70
Jesus Christ, 1, 3, 17–18, 28, 32, 44, 69, 73, 93
Julius Caesar, 73
Justice, 49, 61–62, 74

Kierkegaard, Soren, 55
King, Martin Luther Jr., 78
King, Stephen, 41
Kirk, Russell, 19
Kreeft, Peter, 50

Law, 89
Leadership, 72–80
Leibniz, Gottfried, 84
Leisure, 93–96
Lewis, C.S., 13, 29
Liberty, 30–32, 35–36, 38, 60
Lincoln, Abraham, 77
Liturgy, 29, 64, 68, 71
Locke, John, 36
Logic, 89
Love, 49, 62, 74
Luther, Martin, 37, 73

Magna Carta, 36, 74
Majors, 88–98
Marcus Aurelius, 32, 43, 80
Medicine, 89
Metallica, 21

Subject Index

Middle ages, 2, 3, 6, 41, 44–45, 58, 81, 84–85, 89
Milton, John, 32–33, 36, 38, 51, 61
Montesquieu, 36
Mozart, Wolfgang Amadeus, 21
Music, 82, 91, 95

Netflix, 65, 66
Newman, John Henry, 74–75
Novels, 41
Nursing, 90–91

Oklahoma Baptist University, 11, 12, 54
O'Loughlin, Michael, 94
Optics, 84
Oxford University, 12

Parham, Angel Adams, 78
Pascal, Blaise, 84
Patience, 49, 53–56, 74
Paul, 18, 19, 20, 63, 73, 96
Pericles, 36
Perseverance, 49
Peter, 63, 73
Philosophy, 41–43, 44, 70, 76, 81, 85, 89, 90, 97
Physics, 89
Plato, 2, 31, 41, 49, 50–51, 61, 80, 83, 85, 86, 98
Plutarch, 73
Podcasts, 66, 67
Poetry, 21, 31, 84
Politics, 89
Postmodernism, 20
Prather, Anika, 78
Prayer, 59, 64
Prudence, 49, 61–62, 74
Psychology, 41
Pythagoras, 85

Quadrivium, 3–4, 82, 84–85, 89, 90
Reading, 54–56, 69–70
Reagan, Ronald, 76

Reason, 25, 45
Reformation, 45
Regulus, 77
Renaissance, 6, 41, 45, 81
Roman Empire, 43–44
Roman Republic, 36, 37, 41, 43
Rowling, J.K., 41

Sayers, Dorothy, 92
Sculpture, 43
Secularism, 29, 37–38, 45, 95–96
Selflessness, 49, 59–61, 74
Sertillanges, A.G., 50
Shakespeare, William, 32, 52, 73, 83, 90, 96
Science, 45
Sin, 32–33, 34
Skepticism, 42
Slavery, 30, 37
Smart Phones, 55, 57, 65, 67
Smith, James K.A., 68, 69
Socrates, 50–51, 83
Solomon, 78
Sophocles, 43, 55
Spain, 39
Spark Notes, 54
STEM subjects, 81–87, 89, 97, 101
Stoicism, 42
Studiousness, 59

Temperance, 49, 61–62, 74
Theater, 43
Theology, 5, 18, 26, 89
Thomas Aquinas, 13, 37, 58–59
Thucydides, 36
TikTok, 57, 65
Tocqueville, Alexis de, 36, 74
Trivium, 3–4, 82, 84, 89, 90
Truth, 5
Truth, goodness, and beauty, 2, 4, 22, 30, 53, 76, 79, 87, 100, 101
Turkle, Sherry, 57–58
Twitter (X), 65

Subject Index

United States of America, 39
University of Bologna, 89
University of North Carolina, Chapel Hill, 12
University of Paris, 89
Utilitarianism, 4, 18, 21, 80

Veith, Gene Edward Jr., 92
Virgil, 43, 52, 90, 97
Virtues, 5, 16, 21, 48–62, 69, 90, 97, 103
Vocation, 5, 24, 82, 88–98

Washington, George, 73

Western civilization, 2, 4, 6, 9–10, 29, 35–47, 73, 80, 83
Westminster Shorter Catechism, 1, 28
Wisdom, 3, 15–17, 24, 33, 50–51, 61, 70, 90, 97
Wonder, 6–7, 24, 57, 65
Wordsworth, William, 98
Worship, 6–8, 104

Yale University, 12–13
YouTube, 19

Zoology, 83

Scripture Index

OLD TESTAMENT

Genesis
1:26–27	25
3:5	58
3:19	92

Job
5:7	90

Proverbs
3:13–15	16
9:10	50
9:11	16
16:16	15
22:6	79

Ecclesiastes
3:11	101
4:9–12	33

NEW TESTAMENT

Matthew
4:4	93
6:11	93
6:33	1, 22
22:37	6, 22, 25
22:39	6
	93

Mark
12:30	69

John
8:32	17
8:34	30
14:6	17

Acts
17	73

Romans
1:20	85
12:2	22

1 Corinthians

3:2	96
8:1	58, 63
13:13	61

Galatians

5:1	30
	44

Philippians

4:8	6, 17–22, 71, 94, 96, 104

1 John

1:8	32

www.ingramcontent.com/pod-product-compliance
Lightning Source LLC
Chambersburg PA
CBHW032233080426
42735CB00008B/837